Scars That Ligh

The Formation and Social Role of Wounded Healers

Reverend David Gray

Published by Barnthorn Publishing Limited.

ISBN: 978-1-917120-02-9

COVER ART BY ROB MALTBY

Back in the days when Manchester was plagued with youth-on-youth violence, I was liaising with Greater Manchester Police on behalf of local communities and young gang members as we sought to create more tolerance and harmony across youth culture. Among those I was working closely with were Patsy McKie, who founded Mothers Against Violence in memory of her murdered son, Dory; and Sylvia Lancaster, whose daughter, Sophie, had been murdered when she and her boyfriend, Rob Maltby, had been attacked in a Bacup park by a gang who took exception to their Goth lifestyle.

Also, around that time, I was privileged to be invited by young people to assist with the Queerstianity movement, which affirmed the spectrum of identity and countered hate messages from street evangelists who, in those days, were verbally abusing Jewish, Muslim, Hindu and LGBT+ children on their way to and from school through the city centre.

One Saturday, having helped young people negotiate a venue in which to meet, I was heading for my bus when I noticed that Rob had an art exhibition on at Affleck's Palace. Popping in to view, I was astonished by the power of Rob's art and immediately went back to find the young people, who had been dispersing when I left them.

Soon, I was escorting about a dozen young people into Affleck's Cafe. Noticing one young woman seeming particularly absorbed in one of Rob's paintings, I asked what she could see. I was astonished and deeply moved by her story.

"I know I look about fourteen", she told me. "In fact, I'm twenty-two. I have a rare condition that means I age slowly but will also die young. All my life, I've been in a web of other people's perceptions of who I am. On one hand, my parents have lovingly been trying to protect me, but seem unable to have the conversation about outliving me; on the other I've been bullied mercilessly by other young people who can't seem to cope with my seeming to not to be getting older as they are. When I came across Queerstianity, I found my people, and with them I found myself. Each of them know what it is like to be different: to have red hair, a strange faith, an unusual medical condition or to live beyond the confines of some perceived 'normal'. If I die before I'm twenty-five, at least I'll die in the fullness of who I am, and it seems to me that that would be enough. In this painting, Rob has captured something that I wouldn't know how to express, but which expresses so much for me."

In that moment, I truly understood the power of art.

The cover of this book about wounded healers is a painting by Rob. The moment I saw it, I began to see things in the image. Here is what I perceive: as explored in my 2023 collection of short stories, *Agatha Christmas*, inspired by conversations with people who were grieving. In the collective unconsciousness of humanity, robins are widely recognised symbols of messengers, or even loved ones themselves, visiting from beyond to let us know that they are okay. Here, the robin seems deeply grounded in a living soul. That soul peeps out through the heart cavity of the robin with a single eye which, though moist, sheds no visible tears. The body of the bird, however, has a seeming of an onion, still in its papery skin, a symbol of both tears and multiple layers of meaning. The sun appears like a halo above the bird's head, perhaps signifying its saintly status–yet this is also the hidden head of the living soul. Together, the beloved dead and the wounded survivor are deified together in deep connection. Though a day may come when the bird will fly away, there is a suggestion that the interconnection will be a grounding and wholesome experience for the living soul. What Rob or others see in this painting is for them to know. All I know is that I love this image, and this is how it speaks to me.

I am grateful indeed that Rob has agreed to his image being used as the cover for this book on wounded healers.

Reverend David Gray, 2024.

DEDICATION

This book is dedicated to all of the people who courageously agreed to speak through its pages: all of them characters in my story, as I am a character in theirs. We have all left footprints in each other's lives.

As in life generally, people's stories often overlap as part of a much wider story, so I hope the reader will forgive occasional repetitive threads. I'm usually the observer, the string connecting their pearls. It has been my honour and privilege to meet every last one of them and the many more they represent, but for whom there was not enough space or whose stories are still too raw to be ready to share.

I'm deeply grateful to all who have agreed to allow me to tell their stories. You have each enriched my life by simply being who you are and in responding to personal difficulties in ways that bring healing to others, myself included.

One person to whom I am eternally grateful is my wife, Elaine. It has not been easy for her to live with an Aspie for almost half a century. How many women would care enough about all women, to respond immediately with love and support, when her husband brings home a prostitute who needs help to identify pathways to a safer future? How many, while bringing up their own children, would make space for street children at the dinner table, or take in an infant so that its mother can pull through detox?

For years, Elaine ran a smallholding, supervising offenders who helped her nurture rescued poultry for fresh eggs and grow fruit and vegetables to supply outreach projects with fresh food for the homeless and other vulnerable people.

Now that age prevents either of us from being on the front line, we are grateful for all the lessons honed on the anvil of life. Among those lessons, we have learned that:

- We will not go hungry while we are willing to make an effort to feed others.
- That privilege and entitlement can make someone too weak to

cope when kismet throws a rock on their life path.

- That Francis of Assisi was right when he claimed that every saint has a past, and every sinner has a future.
- We have learned to live to appreciate that those who have abused our good intention, even members of our family, have paid us in the coinage of valuable lessons.

For all of this, as we ascend the mountain, we are grateful, and in a spirit of gratitude we offer these pages as a route map to future promise.

Reverend David Gray, 2024.

CONTENTS

INTRODUCTION

Woundedness is part of the human condition. If we are not born wounded, we are wounded at birth, when the shock of the new life beyond the womb's cave of comfort shakes us to our core, leading most to forget anything that came before that moment when we felt the midwife's slap. Life continues to wound us in many ways as we adjust to separation, through reconnection with the source of nurture as the infant gets to know its mother in a new, bewildering dimension altogether. This process of change carries forward, through separation at the nursery or school gates; onwards towards a role reversal that is marked by early steps towards independence and what, for many mothers, can become a time of 'empty nest longing'. These are wounds of separation that we all know, for we all must undergo them.

Then there are wounds of grief: the death of an animal who has been part of our household, or of a grandparent or a parent. We all know these losses too. Indeed, though they hit us hard, we learn to expect them as part of the cycle of life. But grief takes on a new dimension when death comes in unanticipated ways. I remember feeling, when my little boy died, that there must be some mistake: parents are not supposed to survive their children. Grief can bring an overwhelming cocktail of emotions when a loved one is suddenly snatched away by murder, accident or suicide.

Of course, there are many other ways by which we can be wounded by life: illness, betrayal, bullying, disappointment, natural disaster or war, to name a few.

Swiss psychologist Carl Gustav Jung (1875–1961) was the first to speak of 'wounded healers', who he describes as those who, having dared to delve deeply into their own woundedness, have learned to mine rich veins of insight deep within both their personal and the collective psyche, before returning to the surface with gifts they feel compelled to use to enable others to accomplish their own healing.

In the 1980s, I was a volunteer with a radio project that offered a Rogerian counselling approach to people in crisis. We also assisted those who, having emerged from trauma, were running projects to help others. Through a wide network of wounded healers, people were able to access support with issues such as debt, addiction, illness, child loss and childhood abuse. It is often those, for example, who have loved someone with a rare condition, who themselves go on to raise awareness about that condition and seek funding to address the needs of those affected. Alcoholics Anonymous is one of the best-known organisations that was set up by a wounded healer, which helps others live with their own alcoholism.

Through this part-autobiographic sharing, I hope to help readers gain an understanding of the relay race of lives that takes place when and wherever wounded healers apply their gifts and insights. The baton in this relay race is forged from pure empathy.

Born nine years after the liberation of Paris, my childhood world was peopled by traumatised humanity. Our working-class community in North Manchester where I grew up in the 1950s, was home to soldiers, sailors and airmen who had been demobbed at the end of the Second World War; their wives and families who had suffered during the Manchester Blitz, and rank upon rank of refugees from Poland, Ukraine and other parts of Europe, including Germany. Many were Jews, often the only members of their families to survive the Shoah (Holocaust). Every adult I knew had been traumatised by war, including my own family. My mother, a WREN (a member of the Women's Royal Navy Service), had met my father when they served together in the Royal Navy. My maternal grandfather had fought in the Boer War and then in the trenches of the First World War, where my grandmother fell in love with his dignity masked by a shrivelled body wounded by shrapnel and mustard gas.

In time, my grandparents would send their own children off to war, losing a son when my Uncle Cyril, an RAF Flight Sergeant, was shot down during the Battle for Holland during Operation Market Garden. Aunts, uncles and other family members saw service in the armed forces or, like my beloved uncle Walter, in the Home Guard.

I came into this world with a condition that was not then on the radar of health and education professionals and found it quite bewildering as a child on the autistic spectrum with honed empathy to be surrounded by and absorbing so much anguish. My ability to develop cloaking and coping mechanisms did not develop until much later in life, and as a child I was at the centre of a primal scream.

Amid this turmoil, my regard for those who had lived through one, and sometimes two world wars, began to ripen towards reverence. Years later, the war generation would pull strings to give me the honorary rank of major, so that I could take my place as a veterans' chaplain.

My own wounds were mainly psychological following an encounter, aged ten, when I was poorly equipped to make any sense of it, with a child killer. With my undiagnosed Asperger's syndrome compounded by post-traumatic stress, I became a toxic child, unable to articulate what was going on for me–not least as I didn't know myself.

In sharing how I came to terms with my woundedness, before going on to help found the Lifeshare charity to help others, and to work as a counsellor, therapist, social worker, Christian priest and Interfaith minister; then telling the stories of people I encountered in those roles who were also reeling from the impact of war, homelessness, addiction, mental ill health, child sexual abuse, human trafficking and other traumas that can underlay symptoms of mental ill health and PTSD, I hope to show that some scars enable light to enter into the darkest corners of our human experience.

Most of the stories in this collection, though they inevitably dovetail into one another, stand-alone. After all, like the cosmos itself, all things are connected. Via snippets from my childhood, the reader may discern a process of intergenerational osmosis that slowly equipped me with insights that would reveal my future path through life. Those who persevere will learn how my journey from victim to survivor helped me recognise and assist other wounded healers.

Having negotiated my own passage through the darkness, there was mutual recognition whenever I met others affected by trauma. In a spontaneous combustive sort of way, we became a growing network of those learning to shine our light through the scars.

This is an unusual autobiography, for my own journey through life is told through the stories of others met along the way. It relates how my time in care informed my approaches when working to empower young people leaving the care system; it covers my role as an all-forces padre, outlining battlefield pilgrimages with veterans of two world wars and subsequent conflicts; it relates how I became a negotiator, including during an Easter prison riot that was itself an Easter experience.

Discerning readers will see clearly why it was inevitable that my role in establishing the Lifeshare charity to work with people on the furthest margins of society came about.

Some of these stories were first aired in my weekly newspaper column. Now, along with other real-life stories, they have been linked together like a string of pearls to offer a 'read between the lines' narrative of valuable insights as to ways in which society can improve its attitudes to and responses towards those who are often looked down on, perhaps increasing understanding to reveal that the people we see as needy may have the qualities society itself needs if we are to truly learn from the lessons of history.

In the 1980s, we came across almost a hundred Second World War veterans who had been sleeping rough since being demobbed at the end of the war. That these men were still homeless forty years after being promised a 'country fit for heroes', spoke volumes about the kind of society we had built in the post-war years. It was clear something needed to be done to change things.

If we could truly learn from the lessons of both history and her story, we would soon see how, together, we could make our world safer for women, children and those who become vulnerable due to age, ailment or circumstance. Like white blood corpuscles, wounded healers, having survived trauma and abuse to use their insights to help new generations of survivors, are essential to this process.

The stories are told with a healthy dollop of that vital humour that has, throughout history, enabled fragile human beings to cope in times of extreme stress.

The men and women behind these stories, though often overlooked by passers-by, are revealed in a new light that puts the reader in awe of what they have actually achieved.

One last thing before you, the reader, engage with this patchwork narrative: be ready to move beyond any learned thinking that may lead you to expect a story written from a particular faith outlook. It is true that my own cultural traditions will, along with iconic stories and characters from the Abrahamic faith stories on which I was brought up, influence the language bricks I utilize. However, no sojourner through this life who truly seeks can avoid finding a vast array of gems of great worth in mines of faith, science, philosophy, art and music, as well as all expressions of life.

PART 1

A CHILDHOOD IN 1950S CHEETHAM

The Wisdom of 'Solly' Solomon

Growing up in Cheetham in the 1950s was an amazing adventure! Poles, Jews, West Indians, Christians, Sikhs, Muslims, Chinese–people from all imaginable backgrounds–contributed to the tastes, smells, sights, sounds and textures of my childhood world. Older neighbours, thrown together in the aftermath of the Second World War, having experienced the horrors of fascism, nurtured mutual empathy between people of all backgrounds.

When St. John's Sunday school closed due to dampness, local children found themselves on an exciting journey into each other's faiths for, when he learned about our situation, neighbour 'Solly' Solomon offered his garment factory as a temporary Sunday school. This neighbourliness brought unexpected blessings to local children of all faith backgrounds, and Solly's daughters and their Jewish playmates soon grew curious.

"What do you get up to in Uncle Solly's factory?" asked one of his nieces.

"Come and see", we invited.

The Jewish children's first experience of Sunday school led to the ironing out of one or two misunderstandings.

"That was not so bad", said one of Solly's girls, who admitted to having harboured an idea that her dad's factory would become haunted by a mysterious entity she had heard Christian children refer to as the "Holy Ghost". "It was a bit like Schule."

"What's Schule?" asked several little voices.

"You come and see!" was the reply.

The following week, I was one of several little Christians delighted to receive a spoonful of honey from the Rabbi to show that learning was sweet. By the time that the first Mosque opened, having discovered the delights of visiting each other's respective rooms of faith, Judaic-Christian children were soon angling for an invitation from their Muslim playmates. It was a time of innocence, a time of fascination with each other's different beliefs and customs, a time of sheer wonder. Our talk at play, a combination of Lancashire Twang and Yiddish–the Mame-Loshn of many among us–was of new delights we'd tasted, fresh ideas we'd encountered and of interesting new friends we'd made.

Our friendships were cemented by the food that was always on offer at Synagogue, Mosque, Church, Sikh Gurudwara and Temple. Most of us came from poor families, and our taste buds had never had such adventures as Gefilte fish, bagels and lox, latkes–and the most mouth-watering curries imaginable. I've always felt it a real shame that the church fare rarely rose above tea and biscuits. While we each remained faithful to our personal religious and cultural roots, we were enriched in countless ways by what we shared with and of each other at the meeting place of faith and culture. Years later, the word 'Lifeshare' earned an important place in my vocabulary that was rooted in my childhood friendships. Had the slum clearances not intervened to split us all up, who knows where our adventures might have taken us?

Man of the House

My association with fairgrounds pre-dates my brief period as the Ape-Keeper at Belle Vue Zoo and even my birth. Though I was an adult when I discovered that my paternal grandad ran Gray's Fair, which still tours southern England, I'd no idea as a boy that it was the war that altered my father's course through life. After his wartime stint with the Royal Navy, Dad swapped the fairground traveller life for life at sea. He came to love the sea so much; he began to spend far more time with her than with his family. When I was eight, he left altogether.

From an early age, then, people in those days were telling me that, as the 'Man of the House,' I must support my sea-widow Mother.

Mum worked hard to make ends meet. When she was at 'Austin's Rope Works', Les Dawson's Mum was a colleague and mum swore Les, who had worked there at weekends in his youth, learned the mannerisms of women who had to communicate over the clatter of the loom, which he used to great comic effect in his *Cissie and Ada* sketches with Roy Barraclough. She was also involved in making the nooses for hangman, Albert Pierrepoint. It was years before I realised mum was not offering to take me to the park when, if I was naughty, which was often, she'd say: "Our David, I could swing for you!"

She used to bring home 'ends', tassels and bobbins that afforded me hours of play, just as she'd bring home bags of broken biscuits, or 'brokes' when she worked at CWS Biscuit Works.

Mum had other jobs as a cleaner, working for local cinemas and better-off Jewish families, which in turn led to her cleaning at one of the many local synagogues.

As she was often still working when my little sister, 'Titch', and I finished school or during school holidays, we spent many hours in the care of our maternal grandmother, from whom mum would collect us when she finished work.

Walking home from Gran's, Mum would often mutter, "I've worked my fingers to the bone today!" As a small child, I took this literally, assuming her skin grew back overnight. This increased my resolve to find ways to help her out–though I knew it would shame her if she found out, so had to be careful.

The world seemed safer for kids in those days and it was easy for me to find ways to earn a crust to help mam out. An older boy got me my first job, and at the age of seven, I was delivering coal on a pram from the Coal Yard near Harietta Street to the backyards and cellar grids of Cheetham and Hightown. Being daytime when folk were at work, tips were few and the Coalman rarely remembered to cough up, so I left. Then, while visiting Heaton Park fair during one Easter holiday, a man asked me to watch his slot machine. People were showing interest in his children's carousel, so I started a bit of banter to keep them there until he returned.

"Well lad," he'd said, "you seem to be a natural. Think you can work that thing?"

"Sure, mister!"

I loved that Carousel! Especially the craic with the man on the adjoining pitch!

"There's no seat belts on his rickety ride!" He'd warn the mums and dads, "Mine's new!"

"Don't need 'em!" I'd shout back, "His goes far too fast!"

Perhaps because I was a kid, people queued for my ride. The boss was so impressed he gave me a whole florin at the end of the week.

Years later when working with Henry Hochland, a member of the Hochland family of Haig and Hochland University Bookshop fame (the enterprise was started after the Second World War by a Holocaust survivor who arrived in England after the war as a Kindertransport boy having lost all his family), we were talking about genetic memory. As we had looked through the archives of the Windsor Boy therapists for a book that would explore generational trauma, it suddenly occurred to me that despite knowing nothing of my fairground traveller ancestors as a boy, I seemed to have innate skills that were homed in long before I was born. The fair was seasonal, so before long it was back to the coal. Older and bolder, I insisted on a shilling a week plus tips and was very proud the day the coalman gave me my own barrow.

Slyly slipping my earnings into the pocket of Mum's coat on the back of the door, my heart would swell when, searching for her matches, she'd suddenly exclaim: "Bless me! I've found a half-crown I forgot I had! Run to Brown's our David and fetch us a tin of pineapples and some Carnation milk to have after tea!" One day she caught me putting coins in her purse and accused me of being a thieving little sod, so I had to go easy for a while so as not to blow my cover. The day my cover was finally blown was the day my childhood ended, more of which to come.

Sally Ann

My first seven years of life were spent living at 20 Marsland Street in Cheetham Hill, close to the Chasidim area of Broughton where my home city of Manchester meets its sister 'Sally'–Salford. Where the bottom of our street met Marlborough Road, there was a Salvation Army Citadel. Homeless men, and occasionally women, needing a bed could get a voucher there for one of the hostels in Salford or Town, both within walking distance. They had to pay a token fee, so we regularly had 'tramps'–a term that these men of the road were proud of, for it denoted their stamina as men of the road who tramped the byways of England–knocking on our door holding a small brush and a tin of Airfix modelling paint offering to paint the house numbers in return for a few coppers. By the time they got to the end of the street, they'd usually found enough householders in work to have made what they needed to secure their kip.

As a boy, I really felt for these men, who made me appreciate having a loving mum who kept a roof over our heads. My empathy grew when I overheard remarks my grandfather would make to Gran over my back, as I was preparing the grate for the morning's fire after he came home from his night shifts: "They peeled another poor sod off the kiln this morning, Clarissa." He'd been working nights in the brickworks near Strangeways Prison. Homeless men, many of them war veterans, would huddle around the brick chimney for warmth.

But as the kiln cooled down and night temperatures dropped below freezing, it was not uncommon to find some poor soul dead from hyperthermia as the morning whistle blew to mark a change of shift.

A few years later, we moved to a bigger house in Thirlmere Street across Hightown.

Nearby to this house was a stable where a rag-and-bone man kept his horse. He used to let 'tramps' sleep in the hay loft. There was one old chap who wore a flat cap and a big herringbone coat in all weathers. I'd see him knocking about and always wanted to know his story but didn't know how to ask in those days. He had a big bushy beard that had once been red and looked a lot like one of Michael Bentine's 'Potty-Men'.

Once in my bedroom, after Mum told me off, I spotted him passing. Opening the window and ducking below the sill, I whistled for his attention and started tossing the coins I'd been secretly hoarding for Mum down into the street, where he eagerly gathered them up. Even now I can't be sure whether my motivation was to help him or to spite Mum. Still, what you don't know doesn't hurt you.

Many years after these events, the great-grandson of Salvation Army founder William Booth, Stanley Booth Clibborn, who was then Bishop of Manchester, played a part in my life that persuaded me to seek ordination as an Anglican priest, more of which in due course.

The Scrapyard Spitfire

While making my way home one evening after playing in Elizabeth Street Park, I recall standing in astonishment at the sight of a Spitfire atop a mountain of old vehicles and other metal in the scrap yard at the bottom end of Herbert Street. How could adults allow this to happen? While the word heritage would probably have been strange to me then, my thoughts were that someone was making a huge mistake in consigning this icon of British grit to the scrapheap of history.

That area of Cheetham Hill has changed enormously over the years. The Jewish Hospital has gone, as has the washhouse that used to be across from the scrap yard. Even the Police box has vanished from Marlborough Road–unless the BBC is using it as a prop on Doctor Who. In my childhood, that small area afforded me many adventures.

Some of the larger houses that once stood there had been boarded up for as long as I could recall. In early 1961, I and my playmates climbed over the back wall of one in search of a lost ball. One of the lads was near the rear door.

"Look at this!" He shouted.

In among the weeds and debris, he'd found a rusty Tommy helmet. We were used to finding gas masks, bayonets and such buried on old crofts or in disused garages.

Another lad was looking at the door. "Blimey! That's rotten and rusty. Bet it would open with a shove!"

He was right. Tentatively, we made our way inside. It was amazing! The building had been used to store and issue supplies to British troops during the war. After the war, it had simply been locked up and forgotten. There was a huge desk, its drawers still stuffed with musty papers, inkpads and rubber stamps. Upstairs we found racks of boots, RAF tunics and stacks of blankets. At first, I felt uneasy. But recalling the Spitfire, I told myself adults didn't care about these things any longer and was soon leaping around lost in our games.

Someone found some tubes of red ink, which we had the bright idea of using as play blood. By the time we wended our way home, we were dressed in boots and uniforms far too big for any of us and sporting fake wounds guaranteed to make our mothers wince.

In fact, they inflicted real wounds on us for our getting into mischief, that made us wince!

A few years later in 1967, the Beatles released their *Sergeant Pepper's Lonely Hearts Club Band* album. The famous sleeve image of George, Paul, John and Ringo in Lord Kitchener attire made old uniforms suddenly trendy. How I regretted that by then the abandoned quartermaster's store had been demolished and all trace of its historic content gone to who knows where?

When Welshy's Lad Went Missing

Thinking that adulthood was a disease which made people stupid, I had a boyhood fear of growing up. One early experience taught me that children have their own wisdom and that adults should not assume that theirs is superior. Enabling children to express what they may be trying to say is almost sacred to me now. Adults can learn much from children they are willing to listen to. Here's why I believe this.

When I was about five, Mum answered a knock at the door. A neighbour came bearing bad news. 'Welshy' up our street, while bathing her toddler in the tin bath, had gone to deal with the milkman at the front door. While her back was turned, her lad had vanished. The back door being ajar, she'd been frantically looking for him in the entry.

"Come on, our David", Mum had said, "Get your coat!"

At the scene of the mystery, we found Welshy sobbing her heart out, despite neighbours assuring her they would find her lad. My eyes being on a lower level than those of grownups, I soon spotted something they had missed.

"Mam!"

"Shut up, our David! Can't you see poor Welshy's worried? I'll take him out." In the street we met another neighbour who had been scouring the area.

"He'll not be found alive", she offered sagely, her chin doing a little dance.

More fruitless searching followed. Back in Welshy's parlour, I was again forgotten while the adults shushed the distraught mother. What could I do to get through to these grownups that they were worrying about nowt? My eyes level with the fireplace, I could see into the chimney where two little legs stood atop an unlit grate and a little form, hidden in soot, stood chuckling silently at all the fuss.

Taking a lead from Mum at the nursery gate, I gobbed on my hand and began to wipe away soot. A bloke spotting what I was up to suddenly stole my thunder as he realised what I'd known all along.

"Here you are, Welshy, I've found him for you", he boasted, scooping the child from his hiding place. I didn't know how to swear then, but what I'd thought at that moment translated to something like, "You b*st*rd!"

Back then, children were to be seen but not heard. Why didn't I realise this? On the way home, I made the huge mistake of tugging Mum's coat and saying, "I knew he were there all along, Mam!"

Smacking me a belter round the back of the head, she'd responded, "You little sod! Why didn't you tell us? Couldn't you see how worried his poor mother was?

Great Uncle 'Todger' Jones VC DCM

As I'm fond of pointing out, history is like a Matryoshka doll. World history contains the history of the nations; each nation holds the history of its component communities; each community holds the histories of schools, businesses, and families… and each family holds the history of its individual members. We can be proud of whom who we are connected to and give them reason to be proud, in turn, to be connected to us.

My grandad, Fred Mabbott, rarely spoke of his experiences in the trenches during the First World War. It was from his muckers that I picked up snippets about rat stews and how, by the courtesy of shrapnel and mustard gas, he'd obtained the distinctive scars that covered his face and body. Grandmother Clarissa (née Thornton) was a beautiful woman who cherished the dignity that dwelt within my working class grandfather's battered frame.

Once, when their home hosted visitors from the Runcorn side of the family, I overheard a hushed mention of another relative. Later, Mum told me a little more about 'Todger', who himself, like most veterans I knew in boyhood or have known since, spoke little about his war or how he came to win the Victoria Cross (Britain's highest award for gallantry).

A few years ago, when doing a service for the Cheshire Regiment, the soldiers all wanted to shake my hand because of my family links to Todger, whom they considered to be one of the most important members of their regimental family. It was from them that I learned something of his amazing story.

On 26th September 1916, the 1st Cheshire Regiment was digging-in, having just taken the village of Morval. Todger was talking with his friend, Runner Kenworthy.

"It's a great day, Todger" Kenworthy was saying, "My eighteenth birthday".

His life was ended the next moment by a sniper's bullet. With orders to dig in, Todger leapt up and cried, "If I'm to die today, I'll die fighting, not digging!"

A sniper in a tree put a bullet into his tin hat, where it buzzed round "like a bee in a basin" before dropping, still hot, down the back of his tunic. Firing from the hip, Todger took the sniper out. Despite four further bullets entering his great coat, Todger dealt with two further snipers who'd been using a white flag of truce to hide their murderous intent. Soon, Todger was in among them in the trenches calmly shooting any who posed a threat.

That evening, during the twilight barrage, Todger returned to the British trenches with 102 prisoners. Others had been killed on the way by British shelling, Todger himself receiving a neck wound from this 'friendly fire'.

King George asked curiously: "How'd you do it?" during a visit to Runcorn after the Armistice to award Todger his VC.

If kings can be curious, it does us well to be curious too. What wonders, dear readers, wait to be uncovered in your own family history?

Todger's statue, opposite Runcorn War Memorial, is dedicated to those who came back.

Barrow Boy

1960s folk were used to grime. Adults worked in mines, factories and foundries, while kids played on crofts and in Blitz-bombed houses. All I had to do to hide my coal round from Mum was sneak in the back scullery at Gran's and scrub up before Mum got home from work. The day she found out I'd been delivering coal marked the beginning of the end of my childhood.

It was the school holidays. I'd delivered my last drop of the day on Wigton Street. My grandparents lived up at number 9, and Gran would be busy if I snook into the scullery now. At the other end of the street stood a grocer's shop. I'd been hoarding my tips. Twelve shillings and sixpence (12/6D–62p in today's 'Noddy' money) was a fortune to an adult in those days, let alone to a child. The shop had a sweet counter, where I figured I could get everything a child my age could need in the world for that tanner, and still drip a handsome twelve bob into Mum's pockets.

Parking my barrow, I bobbed into the shop. The shopkeeper looked up from the counter as the jangling bell announced my presence. She'd been leaning across to speak with another woman seated in the chair reserved for honoured customers.

In those days people were patient with children and old people alike. Besides, I was grimed with workers' honest dirt. After a quick glance, they resumed their chat. Should I get a bar of Dairy Milk, Spangles or a bag of Uncle Joe's? I must have stood there for ages, when the woman–who could not be seen from outside but had a diagonal view through the window–spoke to me, "That man seems awful interested in your barrow, lad."

Glancing through the door panel, I spotted Mr Curious. He was young. His smart dark suit said he wasn't local. A white car parked near the kerb confirmed, definitely not a local. We couldn't afford cars!

I stepped outside.

"Hello", making as if he'd just seen me. Coins jingling in my pocket gave him his cue. Smart-ass glanced towards another man sitting in the driver's seat, "We're policemen investigating local meter robberies. We'd like you to come to the station with us."

His accusatory implication made me angry. Pride at my hard earned efforts boiled up in me, probably saving my life.

"If you're a copper, where's your warrant card?"

His next words made the hairs rise on the back of my neck and I could feel rivulets of coal-dusted sweat trickling down my back.

"You watch too much telly, sonny."

Casually, he produced a plastic wallet. The sort I'd seen on the toy shelves of the paper shop window on Marlborough Road when, seemingly years ago, I and my mates had sessions of 'Bags I'. Stepping back, my heel caught the door making the bell jangle. The driver panicked, "Come on, Ian, let's go!"

Smart-ass calmly got into the car, which drove away hastily.

After the bogus police officers drove away, I stood rooted like a rabbit in headlights outside the Wigton Street shop afraid they would return. Somehow, I found the strength to run to Gran's. Forgetting to go around the back to scrub up in the scullery, I leapt up the front steps to tug the bell pull.

Big mistake!

My guilt was written all over my face in grime when Gran opened the door.

"What' you been… just wait 'til your mother gets home! Ungrateful little…" When she'd calmed down, I told her about the men in the car, begging her to call the real police.

"You're ok", she'd said-meaning: "This is a respectable house! What would the neighbours think if the police knocked on OUR door?"

When Gran told Mum, even 12/6D wasn't enough to assuage her shame that her son thought her so poor he'd gone out on the coal.

The barrow was there as we walked home, and there the next day. I felt guilty not returning it to the coal yard, but it was so associated with fear and guilt now that I couldn't touch it.

I stopped playing out and tried to persuade my little sister to stay close to Gran's too. The house, with its garden, bedrooms, parlours, attics, coal cellar and scullery seemed enough adventure to me right then. Sis just thought I was crazy. I was worried sick when she went out, relieved when she returned for meals.

As my confidence slowly returned, I too was playing out again. For maybe he was a policeman and perhaps had needed to go and deal with some real criminals. He hadn't touched me. Were my fears all in my own 'bonce'?

The Day the Music Died

The day my childhood ended; things had returned to normal. Mum had forgiven me. She even seemed to understand I'd been trying to help. Gran, who'd always loved me, was soon telling Mum how one day I'd make her proud.

One day, Gran and I were sitting in the below-stairs parlour when we heard a footstep on the cellar grid followed by the snap of the letterbox. "Go fetch 'paper, our David. I'll make us some tea."

Walking upstairs past the model Hurricane that was a constant reminder of Uncle Cyril, shot down at the Battle of Arnhem, on past the portrait of Gran as a young woman in fine, Victorian clothes, in the landing recess, I stepped down the lobby to the front door. The *Daily Sketch* lay folded on the mat. Reaching for it, my eyes sought the headlines. The man who'd tried to persuade me into that car was staring back at me from the front page. Next to him was a woman with peroxide blonde hair. A few years later, lyrics from Pink Floyd's song *Brain Damage* would remind me of that moment of realisation: "The lunatics are in the hall... the paper holds their folded faces to the floor... and every day the paperboy brings more..."

His name was Ian Brady. The Moors Murders had hit the media.

Reading what he'd done to other children, a slow death crept into my heart. My sense of God's perpetual presence was replaced with guilt. My child's mind convinced me that had I got into the car that day, a worthier child than me might have survived. It was the onset of what, as a veterans' chaplain, I've learned to call survivor syndrome. As a small boy, it manifests as an unshakable sense of self-loathing coupled with deep, seething anger.

My child-self had died by the time I'd handed the paper to Gran. Now began my fall into years of darkness–years in which I could not tell another soul for fear they'd hate me as much as I now hated myself. If I needed proof that I was the most loathsome thing on God's Earth, it was the then unshakable 'fact' that even God could not bear to be near me.

People were judgemental about the Moors Murders.

"He only took kids no one wanted", someone told Mum in my hearing. What an inane comment! Being poor wasn't a crime! How could I tell Mum now? She'd think she'd failed.

For ten long years, I couldn't tell another soul about my inner hell, but my behaviour spoke volumes. If an adult treated me unfairly, with nothing to lose and little to live for, they'd get a vitriolic response. Teachers, Mum, neighbours–anyone who assumed to know what was going on for me, especially those who opined that "it's because he has no father figure", got the benefit of my deep, primaeval growl. To them, I was not a child with a problem, but a child who WAS a problem.

I started to wander off at night. Mum followed me once. She was shocked to find me in Queens Park Cemetery crying at the grave of Mary Helen Summersgill, who'd perished one C19th Bonfire Night. Mum couldn't know I was pleading for this innocent child to live so that I could take her place in the world of the dead. Before long, I'd earned a probation officer. In court one day, a magistrate was outlining a list of my evil deeds, including smashing a bottle of lemonade against a neighbour's wall.

"Is this all true?" he'd asked, offering me an opportunity to explain.

My undiagnosed Aspie self could not lie. "No. It was a bottle of cream soda!"

In the end, after running away to sleep rough, considered "beyond parental control", I was taken into care. Constantly told what a wicked ingrate I was by adults who defined my reality, always an odd child due to being on the autistic spectrum that seemed not to be on the radar then (I was in my fifties when I learned I was an Aspie), I'd become a despicable child who, though nobody dared say it aloud, was unfit to live. Those rare moments when adults didn't fill the gaps in their understanding with off-the-mark theories, allowed the real me to find expression, but these were too scarce to have a therapeutic effect. I suppose they had an accumulative impact, for eventually I found my way back from hell.

The Cream Cake Kid

Once, a residential worker came to my aid when the other kids were bullying me in the orphanage stable. Kids could do anything to me. I deserved their anger for having lived. But when he raised his hand to the bully, what happened next shocked everyone, including me. The other damaged kids gave me a wide berth afterwards.

Picking up a pitchfork, I stabbed out and seriously grazed his leg.

With shocked understanding, he had gently taken my arm and silently limped me back across the field. Our eyes never left each other. There was a deep sorrow in me and a deep concern in him. He helped me because he didn't judge me. He never asked me why I'd reacted like that, but from then on, I knew he knew that there was a real person inside this wicked child. If he knew, perhaps I could learn to know it too.

From the orphanage, I moved to a foster placement and came to love the other kids there. Will, Dan and their sister Harriett had no family looking out for them, while Tina would be going home when her Mum regained her health.

We were made to call the couple 'Mum' and 'Dad'–but 'Dumb' and 'Mad' summed up how they were towards us. There were lots of foster homes in Langley, near Middleton, back then. A van used to come around delivering groceries and the foster homes sent kids out with lists to order food on tick. One day, I waited till the van was several streets away and ran up panting.

"Sorry, mister, my Mam said she needs extra stuff for visitors." With my ill-gotten booty of biscuits and Swiss rolls, I met the others in our favourite hideaway. We scoffed ourselves silly. We usually got moist broken biscuit 'treats', while their own son got the best. 'The Cream Cake Kid' was spoiled and once threatened Dumb with a knife–but Dan got shouted at for taking it off him.

Standing Up for Each Other

Up to now, I'd been like a feral child fighting his corner. Soon, I was to learn that supporting others would serve my own cause too.

When Will got upset, Tina asked what was up. He sobbed out a tale that troubled us all. Dumb and Mad were secretly forcing him to steal materials to do up their own house near Heaton Park. Harriett and Tina went for a quiet chat. When they returned, Tina looked furious. "We've got to get help". I'd no idea what the girls discussed that day. Years later when I had more knowledge of the world, the possibilities made me sick. Tina said she and I had the least to lose as we still had family looking out for us, but Dan insisted "Will's my brother–I'm going". I was so proud of him.

The two of us went the next afternoon. On the pretext of sweeping the yard, we went over the backs and bluffed a free ride on a bus into Manchester. Can't remember the whole of that journey, but we walked up Kingsway–one of the few routes we knew back to the orphanage. The young social worker we met there listened to our story and asked us to trust him and go back. He gave us our bus fare and as it turned out, we were right to trust him.

Back at the house, my Mum was there with our vicar along with social workers and a burly policeman. Mad was going on about Harriett hanging around with bikers. Only a kid myself at the time, it was years before it clicked that he was lying to offer an alternative suggestion for the signs of sexual abuse they might find or that the poor child might one day try to speak out about.

The next day after school, Dumb and Mad were gone. A lovely relief couple looked after us until new foster parents were appointed. Anne was genuinely interested in my love of Edgar Allan Poe and didn't dismiss it as morbid as most adults seemed to. Thus, it was possible to tell her a little about the nightmare landscape of my mind–but not, yet the full story.

When they came, the new folk really cared about us, earning our respect and love. The husband of our foster family had been a prisoner-of-war to the Japanese and had a highly honed level of empathy.

Mr. Payne never spoke about his wartime experiences, but rising early with him when he got up for work, my school being two bus rides away, there was a mutual understanding in our companionable silence, something that needed no explanation. We each knew the other had suffered terribly. Even as a kid, I knew what he must have gone through was far worse than what had happened to me. Simply sharing toast and marmalade with this kind man who had witnessed terrible unkindness helped something inside me begin to settle.

It would be a long time still before my head broke the surface but having stood up to an abusive foster family and then experienced levels of trust with their kind replacements that I had thought never to know again, I was becoming stronger. I was in touch with them years afterwards and believe it was their nurturing that empowered Dan to become a Royal Air Force officer. Will and Harriet achieved good things too.

We were delighted for her when our wise, loyal friend, Tina, went home soon afterwards. A good number of years later, I met her again during an event at Manchester University. She had done well and was helping young families through the project in question.

Satan's Slave

My grandparents, who had always believed in me despite the grief I had caused them, had died. The damage my brief encounter with Brady had caused to my psyche, in particular, still had a hold on me when, as a young teen, I was living alone in their huge house, with Uncle Walter popping in from time to time to check on me. I left school at fourteen with no qualifications and started work almost immediately in a garment factory.

The church youth club I'd attended as a boy was a place where once I'd had friends. Now, it seemed all normal relationships had been blown forever. The only company I felt worthy of was that of other outcasts, from care kids to homeless people and bikers, who formed motorcycle clubs with names like Satan's Slaves, the Outcasts, Nomads and Hells Angels. Somewhere deep inside, part of me realised that I was straying from the path that had once offered me some sort of meaning.

One night, wearing crudely homemade Satan's Slaves colours, I rode my BSA 250 into the churchyard while the youth club was underway. I was wild, drunk, and determined to show the normal kids that they didn't scare me. I wanted to intimidate them. They must know I was out there, as I revved the throttle and sped between the gravestones. There must have been a funeral planned for the next day, as I didn't see the grave that had been dug in preparation and when my front wheel caught one of the planks that had been placed atop of the gaping hole, the planks parted and in I went, motorbike and all. Somehow, I was not too badly hurt–though my pride was deeply wounded when I looked up to see a group of once familiar faces peering down at me.

One of the youth leaders reached down and pulled me out before he and some of the kids led me inside to get me cleaned up and make me a brew. Later, after sheepishly apologising for being a proper idiot, I stepped outside to walk home. A massive flood of emotion seemed to clear some of my cobwebs when I saw my BSA standing there having been cleaned down. The kindness of the youth club members taught me a great deal about unconditional positive regard. A few weeks later, I turned up with four other bikers, who were as quietly pleased as I was to have found a place in the normal world where we were accepted.

The Price of Membership to the Wounded Healer Network

The price survivors of childhood trauma, especially incestual abuse, pay can be very demanding and often leave the wounded healer abandoned by their own families, who would rather believe the abuser than have their boat rocked. Institutions, including the Anglican and Catholic churches, also tend to abandon the whistleblowers and sweep abuse under their magic carpet.

When a documentary aired that featured me and others affected by the Moors Murders in our attempt to stress the importance of finding ways to enable traumatised children to articulate what they are going through in the hope this would reduce levels of abuse and perhaps help address issues that give rise to serial killers in our society, my siblings needed the comfort of denial. It was easier for them to believe my inner child was a liar than turn to face their part in putting that child at risk. As Janet Brooks had hinted, my safe place was among other survivors, where there was no doubt. As a veterans' chaplain, I have learned the importance of keeping company with others who know enough of the terrain someone has been through to be a quiet, affirming, non-judgemental presence that allows a person to appreciate that, "Being yourself whatever the world may do is vital, because those who mind don't matter and those who matter don't mind".

Anyway, as those who matter know, my close call with a serial killer in my childhood left me bewildered with guilt and a sense of worthlessness. Had I not evaded him, surely a more worthy child would have lived. As if he had put a binding spell on me, it was impossible to articulate anything to adults, though it was the adults' sense of higher understanding and assumptions they made about why I was so disturbed that locked me deeper into my personal hell. All sense of divine presence had vanished, then. I'd felt as abandoned by God, as I felt abandoned by adult society. Inside I was screaming. In desperation, I reached out to find those who would protect me–but who now could I trust?

Superstar

St Damian's RC Science College

In omnibus Fidelis – in all things faithful

Ruby Morrell

I am so proud of you for....

Great report Ruby.

Well done

Mrs Kelly

:)

What dragged me back from the brink of implosion and a fall into the vale of no return was a single idea: trust yourself!

Tentatively, I reached out for the future me. Was that person there? Had I got through this? In a mystic place between sanity and madness, an insane idea suddenly made the best sense of all: my future self was there with me.

"I'm here–so, yes, you made it," it seemed to say. My child self was assured.

"Let me tell you", my adult self might add. "There are times in the future when I too wonder and am overwhelmed. It is then that I reach back in time to find you, for it is you who remind me who I really am. It is only because I've never lost you, my inner child, that I have been able to empower many others who have also been hurt, betrayed and worse".

When my inner child asked: "What happens to us?" Adult me might respond: "We, together, become a wounded healer. In days yet to be, your pain became my superpower. Many people pulled through because in meeting you through me, they realised what happened to them was not their fault. Having seen the dragon that others refused to believe in, they in turn became wounded healers who empowered others to defeat it too."

This, then, was the Poesque, Jungian journey into and through my own hell. Only through such a seemingly impossible journey was who I am able to rediscover its own heaven. Once I became my own guardian, I realised the Lord and Lady had never actually gone away.

Sometime in the early eighties while still working for the Catholic church before founding Lifeshare, I was praying with a group of homeless men. We were saying the Lord's Prayer and when I got to the words "as we forgive those who trespass against us", I froze. I thought about the men, many of whom had been brought up in Catholic care homes or had faced traumatic experience as soldiers, and I wasn't sure I could forgive as God is said to forgive or be forgiven that way either.

That session turned into a deeper conversation that saw some of the men empowered to move on with their broken lives and I realised that part of the established church hypocrisy was its habit of spreading guilt and blame among the people it was asking to forgive its priests who had abused Christ's little ones.

But what about me? There was, I realised, someone I had not

forgiven. But who? My training in psychology and psychiatry, particularly around Jungian approaches and the interpretation of dreams, enabled me to go deeper until I had the answer: Ian Brady. The man who never touched me, but nevertheless had stolen my childhood and my family from me. There followed a journey in which we corresponded for a while. But when I confronted him with who I was, sure he would never forget the barrow boy covered in coal dust; certain my offering forgiveness might lead Brady to a well of remorse that might compel him to offer information that could bring relief to members of his victim's families, he retreated. Lord Longford, before his death, had warned me that revealing why I was writing would cut Brady deeply. It cut him so deeply that he went on a prolonged hunger strike. I had not intended to slash him with that knife of grace.

After years of personal work, alongside others whose lives he had impacted far more than my own, I had been able to play a small part in empowering traumatised people who had been abused as children, broken by what they had witnessed in war or otherwise been ignored, put aside, smashed and dismissed. Having found each other, a few of us agreed to take part in that documentary to ensure that the voices of those, especially children, who were still being traumatised today were more likely to be heard; themselves more likely to be believed and abusers, therefore, more likely to be brought to justice.

When a member of my family whom I had not seen properly since our teens saw that documentary, their response pulled the rug from under me. Basically, in their eyes, I was lying about my encounter with Brady; had always been a devil child and if I had met Brady, he should have killed me anyway–which is precisely what I had thought myself between the age of ten and working my shit out.

That journey from trauma to working one's shit out is, by the way, a requirement of anyone who offers themselves as a mental health practitioner or counsellor. Realising that this now wealthy, cocooned person I loved sided with paedophiles and abusers shocked me so much, I reverted to the inarticulate babbling of the victim. Slowly, I realised that they were embarrassed to have grown up with the shame of having a weird brother! For that, I could forgive them. In the 1950s after all, people with learning difficulties and disabilities were hidden away: out of sight out of mind. No one knew anything about Asperger's in those days, so I was just the 'educationally subnormal' problem kid. Forgiveness I could do–but it was no longer possible to allow their toxic presence in my life, partly because while they were projecting onto me, they were ignoring their own potential healing.

Those on the autistic spectrum, Aspies, Savants and others with misunderstood behaviours, often have higher IQs than Einstein. We are the geeks and weirdos whom everyone else tries to convince are malfunctioning when in fact we are higher functioning, which is admittedly scary for those who have no way of understanding our strangeness. But like the prophets of old, who scared the religious, crown and state authorities so much they tended to put those like us to death. My family member clearly agreed with those ancient societies. Though I stand by my conviction that we have to forgive our family members who don't get it, when I posted as much on a Traveller's Autistic page, my comments prompted a strong response from another person.

Our polite exchange led him to write something that, as a wounded healer and therapist I find amazing:

> In faith, interfaith, therapeutic circles people talk about forgiveness a lot. Many say it is essential to personal healing. Being, like you, an Aspie, I tend to toss coins until I've looked at both sides and stood them on their edges, and so came to question this widely held view. Though I'd often felt disturbed by it, I considered an alternative to meek forgiveness. What if, for the sake of other victims, we learn instead of forgiving to stand firm against corruption and bullshitters regardless of how they threaten, bribe or coerce us?
>
> Mahatma Gandhi, Martin Luther King, Jesus and others whom our community recognises as fellow Aspies function at this level that is neither revenge nor submission. Many on the autistic spectrum resonate close to Karma-Yoga, which means action rather than the fluffy bunny stuff that is a fulfilling spiritual diet for many. Those who lived this path include the very saints you chose to walk closest with Francis and Clare. Accept it. Sitting still with angels floating through your mind is not your way. Some will feel intimidated by that–but only because you hold a mirror to their inner nature. You are not perfect. Who is? However, you are at your best when, accepting who you are you accept becoming yourself".

This, to me, seemed awesome. Anyone for an authentic, respectful conversation? My being me should not, in any way, detract from you being you. As the enneagram of Sufi Islam and the Jungian Myers Briggs Type Indicator of Christianity show, we are all different–but we are all of equal value, and when it is able and willing to accept what combines us, society is healthier, happier, wiser, safer and stronger. Even so, what denies us–even, as Jesus indicated, family–must be let go of.

Years ago, I had a conversation with Winnie Johnson, whose son, Keith Bennett, was among Brady and Hindley's victims. His body has never been found. She had come to find me during a Christmas outside broadcast we were doing on Gorton Market and invited me to her home. Sitting in Winnie's parlour, she talked about her grandson Tony. I'd long known about his murder but had never realised Tony White was a member of Winnie's family. For years I'd dreaded meeting anyone who had suffered at the hands of that pair, fearing they would despise me for having survived Brady's attempt to pick me up, so when Winnie sought me and invited me round for a chat that Christmas around the time of the restoration of the monastery, I was on hallowed ground.

Winnie had heard about my role in seeking to reduce youth-on-youth violence in the gang culture of the time. We had a good natter. I found her wise and kindly. She was upbeat about going to bingo that evening.

Winnie spoke of having worked with a member of Hindley's family and her colleagues making vindictive remarks, which Winnie firmly squashed by telling them, "They may be related to the person who murdered my son Keith, but they are not them. Why would I want to hurt them?"

When she mentioned Tony, I went very quiet. She had looked at me leaning into the arm of the sofa where she sat with another of her grandsons. "Out with it!" She had encouraged.

"It's just that the Penny Black pub where Tony had been murdered had been built on the site of my grandparent's house in Wigton Street, where I had run after Brady was driven off by his mate after approaching me as I stood at the sweet counter of the shop further down. It was also the house where I realised who Brady was and what he had intended, the day I went to collect the *Daily Sketch* as it was pushed through my Gran's letter box and saw his face and the first accounts of the murders."

Winnie was lovely. She was also very feisty, a typical no-nonsense 'Manc' matriarch. She was so unlike the woman the media portrayed; far bigger than the one-dimensional grieving mother they wanted to write about from time to time to titillate their readers' morbid interests via the narrative of the murders they wanted to keep under their reigns. It was partly this media clutch on how the whole thing was viewed that had made it hard for me and other kids who had survived to find an adult with enough common sense and basic human compassion to listen to the insights we could have offered society. No wonder many of us found a path through life as wounded healers, empowering other traumatised children by turning our egos off to actually listen to their hard-to-hear voices.

The Penny Black is now a mosque. My grandparents would like that it has been reclaimed as a place of prayer and kindliness.

Rubber-necking is that strange phenomenon of behaviour that some human beings do when driving past a road traffic accident. They want to see what's happening.

Why?

If the paramedics are in attendance and you've nothing constructive to contribute–move on! Not only are you not helping by hanging around, but you are also contributing towards a tailback that is slowing traffic flow and may even be impeding those who are there to help.

For years, the families of the Moors Murders victims had been subjected to another form of curiosity that, like rubber-necking, offered nothing useful to those who were hurting and, in fact, compounded their hurt. It wasn't just the morbid fascination of members of the public that laid siege to those living on with the pain, but an often-indifferent media that fanned that morbid curiosity by its callous stereotyping of those reeling from and dealing with unfathomable grief.

In telling his story in his book, *If Only*, Terry West, whose sister Leslie was murdered by Brady and Hindley, offers society an opportunity to mature in its attitudes towards crimes of inhuman violence; revealing a way for all of us to move deeper into an understanding of the unintentional cruelty that can occur when people allow their curiosity to become an intrusion on those recovering from trauma.

Another piece of cosmic serendipity arose when I worked alongside a housing officer in a counselling project. To avoid the morbid rubber-necking of unhealthy minds that were maintaining a disturbing egregore among other residents, she had decided to demolish the house at Wardle Brook Avenue where Brady and Hindley had murdered their last victim, Edward Evans.

She remains a friend. Occasionally, I run Laughter Yoga sessions with her daughter.

Doorway to Insight

The next breakthrough came when the slum clearance program got underway, and people's homes were being compulsory purchased. Realising what little security I still had left over from childhood: that my precarious hold on the only community I'd ever known, was about to be taken away, I became suicidal. I confided in a mate that when I went home that night, I planned to end my life. He saved my life by expressing a truth I had not expected to hear. "You selfish bastard!" he had responded. "How do you think the rest of us would cope knowing you couldn't deal with things?"

In his way, he was telling me that I mattered to him. That got through far clearer because he spoke a truth most people would have tiptoed around. Instead of taking my life that night, I resolved to find a way to regain some control of it. All night, I wrestled with my darkness. God was still absent, as I could see not the slightest vestige of usefulness in the God I had trusted as a child having crushed me by allowing Brady to kill children or to come anywhere near me. It was down to me to sort this out. If I didn't find myself a career, I'd end up homeless very quickly once Gran's house was forcibly taken away.

My teachers' view of me as a disruptive, educationally subnormal child had defined my view of myself. Ken Marks, my headmaster who went on to become a Labour MP, had told me: "Gray, if you're lucky, you'll be a dustman". I was never lucky, though it is a job I'd have loved when we used metal bins and were far better at recycling, reusing and restoring.

That night, as a suicidal teenager, I was struggling with my light and dark. The embarrassing sibling in my family, the odd child, having, now, decided to live, something else pinged in my brain, a small smattering of self-worth that told me: "You can't be all that stupid, you can read and write".

Realising I'd never be able to afford a home of my own unless I upped my educational or professional qualifications, it became evident that a new job was required.

But what, and how would I find it? Thinking of my hero, Edgar Allan Poe, himself a troubled child, youth and adult, ideas began to surface. People seemed to think of Poe's world as a dark place of death, horror and misery, but he had also written astonishingly beautiful stories that laid the foundations for modern detective fiction and science fiction, inspiring authors from Arthur Conan Doyle to Jules Verne. In meditation, I invited Poe to sit with me, and I asked for a clue as to what to do next.

"Where were you most content at school?", the genius author's essence asked.

My mind ran through the art studios, metalwork and woodwork classrooms; the gym; the Clough in which the school was set; Maths, English (I loved English literature)–but it was a while before my focus came and found a slightly younger self curled up in the school library one afternoon reading Jack London's *Call of the Wild* in a single sitting. Then, I knew, I had to first become a librarian to gain access to endless supplies of books that could help me identify the path I must take.

The cosmos has a way of adjusting our path according to where we are in logical steps rather than cosmic leaps. Being a librarian was out of reach–but within weeks of my decision, I was working in a city centre bookshop. Our ideals are like stars that we can never reach, but like mariners with the stars, we chart our courses by them.

I was given the religious section, which consisted of a limited selection of prayer books and bibles. I began to add books from Hinduism, Islam, Buddhism, Judaism and then Paganism, Mysticism, and the Occult–and the footfall in that shop increased as rabbis, imams and a whole range of scholars and seekers came to browse and buy books that were not, then, widely available.

My learning expanded enormously, and, after a few rather scary beginnings, I was teaching myself to dream lucidly, making wary expeditions into the astral realms and exploring the splendours of the forest of faith and magic.

Inevitably, I came across the work of Carl Gustav Jung and, though getting there took some very unexpected turns, at the age of nineteen I enrolled as a student at a large psychiatric teaching hospital that had evolved out of a Victorian workhouse.

It was during a class on forensic psychiatry that something the tutor said sent me into a mental meltdown. Charlie Booth was a charismatic teacher, a sort of cross between C.S. Lewis's *Puddleglum* and J.R.R. Tolkien's *Tom Bombadil*, a long-limbed man who looked and smelled like someone who had smoked all of his life. We all looked up to him; hung on his every word, but when he held up *Beyond Belief*, a book about the Moors Murders, and suggested that we read it, my inner clockwork started to malfunction.

"Sorry, I can't read that", I stated with what I now know was Aspie defiance. Charlie, who believed that pushing someone's buttons when they are stressed but unable to explain why might tip them towards a useful insight, looked at me casually and said, "We will be going across to the main hospital tomorrow to listen to the tapes Brady and Hindley made of Leslie Anne Downey's last moments."

Luckily for both of us, and possibly the whole class, the head of the faculty, Janet Brooks, wandered in carrying a stack of books for our reading list. Nobody seemed to notice as she instantly took stock of the situation, plonked the books on my desk and invited me to help her carry them back to her office with a casual: "Silly me. I seem to have brought the wrong books."

Once in her office, she invited me to sit down. I can't recall what words she used to unlock the gate I'd placed on that thread from my childhood, but I found myself spilling the whole story. When I'd finished, I offered to do the decent thing and leave mental health training behind.

"And deny others the benefit of your insights as a wounded healer?" She had countered, before going on to explain how wounded healers were those who have had narrow escapes and lived through a traumatic experience, often emerging with insights that can help others going through similar terrain.

"It's why old soldiers meet at the Royal British Legion and chat over their beers", she said. "Who else can possibly know what they have been through? Their minds are safer in the companionable silence of each other's company than they could be in the company of therapists."

She held the space in which we sat with her kindness.

"Look, we're a teaching hospital", she said at last. "A therapeutic community working with people who have been through various versions of hell. Some have survived war, others the Holocaust, yet others abuse closer to home. They can't always tell us what has happened to them or how they are responding to it, but every one of them has the key to unlock at least some of the doors that are keeping them trapped in prisons of their own minds. That's why we recognise that it is not always the learning of the psychiatrist, the psychologist, the doctor or the nurse that makes the link that enables them to begin their own healing. It might be a conversation with one of the cleaners or another patient that helps them find healing. Your decision–but in my opinion our profession needs people like you. At the least, this training can skill up people like you to be wounded healers in the world."

There was a shift in me that day and I decided to finish my training. The dropout rate was high. Of the twenty students who began together, only four of us completed the course. Others left or decided to shift towards less demanding professional qualifications. In my book *The Great Apes of Belle Vue*, I outline how a goat proved such an effective therapist that I went to work with primates to understand better the benefits of animal companions along life's journey.

So, I moved on along life's path. As I did so, my wounds slowly healed–though the scars will likely always be part of me.

Some of the stories that follow show how my own woundedness helped others heal, while others introduce the reader to other wounded healers I have encountered, including many who got caught up in the fallout of Brady and Hindley's mind-numbing evil, offers society an opportunity to mature in its attitudes towards crimes of inhuman violence; revealing a way for all of us to move deeper into an understanding of the unintentional cruelty that can occur when people allow their curiosity to become an intrusion on those recovering from trauma.

Discovering and Embracing My Superpower

Years later, our team took over a primary school whose pupils were relocating and turned it into a community hub while we raised £6.5million to restore St. Francis Monastery in Gorton. We called it 'The Angels Centre' and ran community art groups; a play resource facility; hot meals for the housebound and other community empowerment initiatives.

Manchester Education rented part of the building back from us to house their special needs team, which is how I found out that I was an Aspie. It used to amuse me to enter my office next to a foundation stone that announced the school had been opened by my old headmaster Ken Marks. I'd loved to have been able to have a friendly chat with him now.

One day, one of the teachers, whose own son was an Aspie, said, "David, you are one of the most gifted community activists I've ever met. People of all ages see you as someone who can get things done. However, I've noticed that you never wear the same pair of shoes twice in a week and that during meetings with powerful decision-makers, you start telling jokes if someone starts speaking over the wisdom of others. Also, you seem to need to have many different things going on in your working life, as you get bored easily. Have you ever been tested for Asperger's?"

"It's interesting you should ask", I replied. "Years ago, when I was a trainee mental health student, we all had to have an IQ test. I did not believe the psychologist who told me my IQ was akin to Einstein's, at that time preferring to wallow in the low expectations of my own teachers. It was easier to think he was patronising me than to embrace it as a fact. But the thought stuck, and years later when I was a social worker, just for the hell of it, I sat the Mensa exam. It astonished me to know that I was in the top 1% and that Mensa itself was full of adults who, as kids, were told they were stupid. There were dyslexic, autistic folk and Aspies among them. Many Mensans, like me, felt they had found out too late that the 'problem' others saw was, in fact, their superpower. What's to lose? How could I find out?"

"I could test you, if you agree?"

It was so agreed, and I was pleased to see her face light up with a big smile. We sat in her office a couple of days later and she told me the results showed I did indeed have Asperger's syndrome. It felt like a relief to know that I just functioned differently. It explained so much. It occurred to me that it may have been my Aspie empathy radar that protected me the day I met Brady.

When my friend started to cry, I asked what was wrong.

"Knowing you are an Aspie gives me hope", she said. "My son is on the spectrum as you know, and all the expert opinion I'm asked to absorb and buy into says that those on the spectrum have no empathy."

"Well, it can sure seem that way when a kid who doesn't realise other children have to hear the same lesson several times before it sinks in can be seen as not caring about their education when they become disruptive", I suggested. "That's often interpreted as their being sluggish, they don't care about the other kids learning. But maybe we have a sort of cosmic empathy that sees a bigger picture. Maybe we can pick up negatives in our educators and become defensive. But over time, we do realise that we function differently, and then we can stop taking it all personally and appreciate that others, from their very different perspectives, have similar goals and aspirations."

"I was so worried about my son's future", she confided. "I'm not anymore! We both know that the only expert on a life is the person living that life."

After that, I was invited to run workshops in schools with children with what was perceived as challenging behaviour. Working together as equals, we were able to help teachers and kids to realise that they needed each other and could have an amazingly positive learning and working environment if they could improve their understanding of each other's needs.

PART 2

BEGINNINGS OF RECOVERY

Poof in the Park

Like most people my age, I've done things and held attitudes that I came to deeply regret. In my teens, for example, I recall a day when having walked from Cheetham Hill to my mate's house in Harpurhey so the pair of us could schlep across to Platt Fields Park to meet with a mutual girlfriend. The three of us had completed an experiment in narrative poetry, which involved one of us starting a story in verse, passing it on for the next instalment to be written by one of the others until it had been round the three of us several times. We all had very different writing styles and wanted to see how these might dovetail into each other. When the poem *The Hermit* had reached completion, we had agreed to meet to discuss the result.

Seated around a rustic table with ice creams and coffee beside the lake in Platt Fields Park, we were chatting away when I noticed an elegantly dressed older man. Wearing a battered fedora hat and a silk cravat at his throat, he minced past our table.

"Bloody poof!" I muttered.

A moment later, he was sauntering past again.

"He's wearing make-up!"

"So, what's the problem with that?" my companions asked.

The more I commented on his presence–the more present he was. He never said a word but had clearly picked up that I was not as mature as my two companions and was calmly walking past to get a reaction.

At first, I fumed. But slowly, it dawned on me that he had every right to be there and that my reaction was the problem, not him. It struck me that he was really brave. He was stating what, deep inside, I, a kid riddled with incorrect labels, felt: "Whatever you think of me, I am who I am and have as much right as anyone to express my personality, sexuality, faith–my whole way of being.

As deep shame seeped into my core, the man seemed to realise he'd made his point and went off across the park.

"You do realise that was Quentin Crisp?" my mate asked.

That day, Quentin Crisp, a man who had stood his ground in far more difficult situations than facing the prejudice of my teenage self, gave me a masterclass. It was one of the best lessons of my life, for I was forced by his quiet presence to take a look at my own prejudices. A great life lesson from a master.

Every saint has a past, and every sinner has a future. I am grateful to the *Naked Civil Servant* for a lesson that has opened my life to the celebration of diversity. Manchester, the city in which Quentin died in 1999 aged 90, is a great place for people to realise the beauty that connects us all across the various spectrums of the human condition.

The Fuhrer's Fury

Intrigued, while restoring Gorton Monastery, by references to an early chapel, we were resigned to never learning its location. In fact, it had been right under our noses all along, emerging during the restoration of the friary into which my thrifty Franciscan forebears had incorporated it once the church was built. Its gothic arches bricked in and floors added, it had vanished under plaster like a magician's illusion.

As a member of Manchester's magic ring, the Order of Magi, I appreciated this enormously. Protected beneath wooden cladding awaiting further restoration, the chapel reminds me of Churchill's War Cabinet magicians, some of whom I was lucky enough to have conversations with as a war generation padre. It was these folk who kept Britain safe from invasion after the evacuation of the British Expeditionary Force at Dunkirk, by creating aerial illusions of fleets where there were no ships or non-existent massed armour. They also hid airfields from Luftwaffe reconnaissance and created clouds over the Thames that hid prime targets during the London Blitz.

It had been in my youth, when I worked as a bookseller's clerk, that I first learned of such tactics from occult author Dennis Wheatley, whose novels such as *The Devil Rides Out* and *The Haunting of Toby Jugg* were often made into films.

One of the roles of our partnership of three bookshops: Sherratt and Hughes in St. Anne's Square; W.H. Willshaw, where I worked in John Dalton Street and university bookshop Haig and Hochland was to host the 'Meet the Author' lectures at the Library Theatre in Central Library.

The authors would often arrive by train at Oxford Road station, where a member of staff from the bookseller hosting their talk would meet them off the train, take them to lunch then escort them to the Library Theatre to deliver their talk as part of a book signing.

Among those I had escorted in this way were Labour politician George Brown; prime minister Harold Wilson's wife, Mary; George Segal, who had written *Love Story* on which a popular film of the day had been based and local author, Alan Garner, whose children's books set in Manchester and Alderley Edge had been great favourites of mine growing up. I'd had flu the day I had been due to meet J.R.R. Tolkien, and not wishing to bump off my favourite author of the *Hobbit*, *Silmarillion* and *Lord of the Rings*, had phoned in sick after asking a colleague to step in. That had led the great man to hand her a leather-bound copy of *Lord of the Rings*, which he had signed, to pass on to me in gratitude for considering his welfare.

Despite having helped Wilshaw's to turn their drab religious section into a beliefs and occult collection of books on all the world faiths, including Paganism, Zoroastrianism and Wicca, occult fiction was not something I found appealing. However, on meeting Wheatley and learning how occult psychology and Jungian research into the collective psyche or subconscious had played their part in leading Hitler a merry dance, avenues opened in my learning that would lead me, a few years later, to enrol as a student at one of Manchester's mental health teaching hospitals.

Over dinner and after escorting the great man across Albert Square to hear him speak, I realised I was experiencing a masterclass from a genius!

Wheatley, you see, did not speak of his fiction, but of his role during the Second World War, when he was the only civilian directly commissioned to serve on the Joint Planning Staff of the War Cabinet. For three years during what was perhaps the world's darkest time, Wheatley had served as one of Winston Churchill's staff officers. That memorable afternoon, I was privileged to hear a master talk about his role in helping the Allies develop methods for using Hitler's obsession with the occult to develop strategies that would influence German troop deployment and have Nazi high command running a wild goose chase.

Tactics like Operation Mincemeat, in which a bogus Major Martin, 'The Man who Never Was', was created to divert attention from the Sicily landings are now legendary.

Exploiting existing legends and inventing new ones, that were authenticated with cleverly convincing antiqued documents 'hidden' where the nazis were likely to find them in art galleries and museums across Europe, the foundations were being laid for future film franchises like *Quatermass* and the *Indiana Jones* stories.

These carefully crafted and craftily placed myths based on plausible Germanic folklore and Märchen like the *Holy Grail*; the *Skulls of Fate*; the *Ark of the Covenant* and the *Spear of Destiny*, all purporting to offer whoever possessed them untold power, had Hitler spending energy searching for such relics. Dan Brown fans will be familiar with the fascination such themes hold for the average mind, let alone the psychotic ego of a madman.

One of my favourite ploys involved releasing thousands of pigeons, each with tinsel tied to its legs, from the back of a bomber during a Berlin air raid. This played havoc with German radar, confusing the mind of a Fuhrer convinced that legendary sky demons that he might harness for his schemes could manifest at any moment.

Like puppet masters, Wheatley and his colleagues cleverly helped shift Hitler's egregores into cocktails of fearful false promises to give the Allies time to muster the push for world freedom. Alongside the work of the Bletchley Park code breakers; S.O.E. (Special Operations Executive) and resistance movements, this approach laid down foundations for psychological strategies that would come into their own during the Cold War when, the old joke goes: "Russia ordered a batch of condoms from the USA with the elasticity to stretch over a 14-inch member. The Yanks sent them back marked small."

Bloody Opera

John Lee, a colleague at the bookshop I worked in as a teenager, once persuaded me to work evenings and weekends for a fortnight at the Palace Theatre on the basis that I'd meet my childhood hero Conrad Phillips, *William Tell* in the 1950s TV series.

Sadler's Wells Opera Company was performing different operas each evening over the period, culminating in Wagner's *Der Ring des Nibelungen* at weekends, in which diva Rita Hunter played *Brünnhilde*, the role that would immortalise her just a few years later. My job as dresser to the male chorus involved getting costumes and props ready between acts, taking my cue from a speaker that relayed the stage performance into the dressing room.

The male chorus could be quite boisterous at times. Once during *Oedipus Rex*, they were cursing about having to crouch on stage disguised as rocks moving in a mist to haunt the ante-hero. Suddenly the door burst open, and Rita Hunter made her formidable presence known: "Gentlemen!" she had chided, "your language is atrocious! Not only is the female chorus up the corridor, but..." she turned a kindly smile on me… "this poor lad cannot be used to such plain Anglo-Saxon!"

Little did she know!

The dressing room went very quiet after she left, the men sitting in front of long mirrors applying makeup. Their nervous silence was suddenly broken by one of the Welsh chaps.

"Nobody bloody understands opera, anyway!" he said. We could sing anything, and the British public would think it was artistic bliss!"

This raised a few giggles, which encouraged him to begin to sing in his beautiful baritone voice: "Bollock to you! You have a face that looks like crap! It hangs like snot beneath your cap…"

As bass and tenor voices started to add harmonies, I began to think he was right. It really did sound beautiful–though I was laughing my socks off as they got into their stride, releasing all their previous negative tension.

Suddenly he called for hush and the singing stopped: "I'll tell you what", my Welsh friend said looking my way with a twinkle in his eye, "after you fetch us some beers, how about you go and be a bloody rock for me and give me a break? Just don't trip anyone up and no bugger would know, see!"

The others thought this a great jape and in no time at all had bribed me to take up the suggestion with offers of a florin or so a piece if I pulled it off. I earned more dosh in my teens than I ever have since!

John Lee, your soul has now gone to the great opera house in the sky, but I'm still grateful that, however unintentionally, you arranged for my first stage appearance–even if no one had a clue until now that

I once appeared with arguably Britain's finest opera company!

Springfield–From Workhouse to Hospital

The site of Crumpsall Hospital–or North Manchester General Hospital, as it has been renamed–has a long and very interesting history that goes back to 1868 with the building of a workhouse to house the destitute. In due course, three distinct hospitals emerged on the site: Crumpsall, the general hospital; Delaunay's, what was in those days called a geriatric hospital where older people were cared for, and Springfield, the psychiatric hospital.

When, at the age of 19, I applied to become a student psychiatric nurse at Springfield, a whole world of personal and community history was to open up to me. The prides and prejudices of my parents and grandparents' generation were nowhere more poignantly revealed than in the hospital complex where local people, as well as being born, healed and nurtured, sometimes died and in some cases were interred according to the understanding of the day as to what constituted 'normal' patterns of well-being and behaviour.

By the time I left the hospital in 1977 to become Great Ape Keeper at Belle Vue Zoological Gardens, my mind, eyes and heart had been opened up by encounters with those who represented the living history of our city.

After our six-week induction training in the school, we students were deployed to work on wards for three-month stints before returning to our academic studies. In our second year, we did three months each on a medical and a surgical ward at the general hospital, but in the main our placements were in wards specialising in various aspects of psychiatry or being out and about visiting people at home with the community nursing teams.

We also spent time in therapeutic departments where art and music were tools of healing or patients were offered work experience in carpentry shops, the hospital laundry, a tailor's department that made nursing uniforms or with the gardening team that helped maintain the hospital grounds.

The fact is most of us suffer some form of mental ill health at some point in our lives. In those days, there was much stigma attached to mental illness and people were often shut away from everyday society for the most bizarre reasons that reflected more on society itself than them personally. For example, it shook me to the core to meet elderly women who had become institutionalised after being admitted for psychiatric care in their youth for no other reason than that they had become pregnant out of wedlock.

Can you imagine being perfectly sane and your peers locking you away because, rather than examine their own attitudes and limitations; it is easier for their consciences to label you as mad?

One poor soul I encountered is someone whose story I will never forget. One day, I was asked to take a message to a locked female ward that we male nurses rarely had access to. As the staff opened the door after I had rung the bell and I began to speak, a middle-aged woman came shuffling towards me. She was frail and had long dark hair. There was something more than the teddy she was clutching that gave her a childlike appearance.

"Tzadie!" she cried, excitedly, adding comments in Yiddish that conveyed her belief that I was indeed her grandfather. The poor soul was convinced that her Tzadie had returned to fetch her home to be with the whole family. She wept inconsolably when she was led away to the day room.

In the office, after I'd given my message to the sister, I wept too as the staff nurse explained that my voice had somehow reminded the poor woman of a world she had once known before the Nazis came and murdered all her loved ones, leaving her a child alone and without hope, her mind shattered by the horror of their hatred.

At the end of my training, the bogeyman of institutionalisation was being used by the Thatcher government as a reason to close down such large institutions and roll out 'care in the community' to replace them. But as I was to discover only a few years later, many people were to sink deeper into misery because of the way this fine-sounding programme was implemented.

When we founded Lifeshare in 1984, it was partly as a response to the fact that mental health had then become a major factor in street homelessness, and we wished to counter a trend that was allowing vulnerable people to fall off the margins of society.

The Goat Therapist

Ward Two was a secure ward, behind which Ken Barnes' smallholding project was situated. The doors of the dayroom opened up into a garden courtyard where goats grazed and chickens, rabbits and other small animals were housed. It was considered that those on this ward were too fragile and vulnerable to enjoy the freedom of entering the wider world without staff supervision. 'Jim' was a patient in Ward Two. He was a very agitated man, who would walk from one end of the ward to the other like a caged lion.

Even at mealtimes, Jim's walking would continue. He'd pause just long enough to take a mouthful of food from his plate before walking off again chewing his meal. It was very difficult to get eye contact with Jim and the last time he had spoken to another human being had been many years earlier. How to engage this once gifted and articulate man was a conundrum most students pondered.

One morning, I came onto Ward Two to commence a shift. It was very early, and most people were still in their beds. The doors to the courtyard being open, I went out onto the small veranda and started to stretch. After a moment, I spotted someone milking a goat over to my right. What happened next was to inform my professional practice as a nurse, counsellor and social worker for the rest of my working life. It was a seminal point in my unfolding calling as a Franciscan and as a priest. The person milking the goat was Jim.

What made me realise that I was standing on a sacred threshold was the fact that he was talking gently and reassuringly to the goat. Had I leapt down and tried to engage Jim in conversation, he'd probably have retreated. What I did was walk slowly to the other side of the goat and crouch down.

Jim was on the right side of the goat, milking it with his left hand while gently stroking its ear with his free hand. He was speaking softly to reassure the animal of his good intention. Moving carefully, so as not to startle either Jim or the animal, I crouched on the goat's left flank and began whispering reassurances into its other ear. "All done", I heard Jim say. Peering across the goat's head I found myself looking directly into Jim's eyes and realised he was talking to me. This was a precious and delicate moment. Whatever I did next could have lasting implications either way.

"Fresh milk", I found myself saying, "That calls for a brew. Fancy a cup of tea, Jim?"

Jim had smiled and nodded. We rose and walked back into the ward together, and Jim stayed with me in companionable silence while I made us both a brew in the ward kitchen. That day was the first step in Jim's long road to regaining his social skills. When I last heard of him, Jim was living in a house with a group of people who had been long-term patients. He was relearning half-forgotten skills, such as how to use a washing machine and do his shopping. Two cats and a very lively dog also lived in that house.

Within a year of Ken starting that smallholding, it was decided that the doors of Ward Two no longer needed to be locked and people, some of whom had lived there in the days when the hospital was still a workhouse, found their lives opened up to a variety of new experiences, from regular attendance at art therapy to small jobs in the hospital or the wider community.

As my final exams drew near, I realised that to improve my qualities as a healer of people it was essential that I had regular contact with and a deeper understanding of other animals.

Keith Bennett's Memorial Service

On 5th March 2010, Manchester Cathedral partnered with St. Chrysostom's, where Winnie Johnson was a congregant, to host a memorial service for Winnie's boy, Keith Bennett. Keith's body has not yet been recovered since he was taken from his family and murdered by Moors Murderers Ian Brady and Myra Hindley.

Many across Manchester were impacted by those terrible events, particularly those living in Longsight and Gorton in the 1960s when the crimes occurred during the upheaval of the 'slum clearances' that split communities and fragmented extended family connections. People were so caught up in the trauma of moving away from familiar neighbourhoods into strange ones, their anxieties increased by the decline of industries that had once offered secure employment, that things were bottled up that needed to be said. It has taken our communities a long time to recover from that combination of events. Some wounds are still raw.

It wasn't just those living through the events that were impacted. Subsequent generations of inner-city children were damaged too.

Tensions between parents wishing to protect, and children who had no idea where anxieties around freedom to play originated, affected a shift in the natural empathy that had long existed between the generations. Crucially, when play facilities ceased to be a political priority, children were growing up in a climate in which play had almost been criminalised and childhood demonised.

Community activists who knew what was happening to their beloved neighbourhoods repeated the message that 'childhood matters' until a new generation of politicians heard and began nurturing intergenerational approaches that began healing the woundedness.

Keith's service offered an opportunity for people of all faiths and none to approach closure about long-standing hurts. Winnie had become the icon of a pain felt by many. Among others I had come to know was a woman who learned that she had been an intended victim as a small child; the man who felt years of guilt for once having had a crush on Myra Hindley, a woman who turned out to be a child killer; myself, whom Brady tried to take when I was ten years of age. Coming together to honour Keith was our opportunity to hold each other in empathetic respect; our chance to say no to all levels of violence against individuals and families; a lifting of burdens that liberated us to stand together to rebuild peace across our city.

As the egregore shifted, we took our chance to expel a fog that had lingered far too long over our neighbourhoods. At last, our love for Winnie and others impacted by his crimes could break the fragile hold Ian Brady had long sought to maintain on his living victims.

At the service, having survived the moors murderers' attentions and intentions as children, myself and others who have spent our adult lives trying to put something good back into the void their terrible crimes left in our communities, lit candles for all victims, living and dead, of the Moors Murders.

As we waited for the service to begin, I caught sight of a man who looked hesitant, as if he was unsure, he should be here. It was clear he too had been, somehow, affected by this far-reaching trauma. Going over to him, I invited him to join us. He told us he was a relative of Winnie and had not been present when Keith went missing as he was in the army. He felt terrible guilt that he hadn't been there and had been unable to face Winnie since. As he told us this, I spotted Winnie coming into the cathedral.

"Come with me I said. Bet she'll be pleased to see you".

Perhaps because he had spoken of his sense of having failed, he realised it had not been his fault at all, just circumstances. Together, we approached Winnie. As they embraced in an emotional and long overdue reunion, I returned to my seat.

Winnie has gone to her rest now. Her service at St. Chrysostom's marked the end of an era–but it also laid down a challenge for society to take steps to protect children, all of us, from the depravities of those who have stepped out of their humanity.

Stepping Stones

For many years, I tried to write all this as a single narrative. But my Aspie mind doesn't work like that. Besides, the telling has grown as my path has crossed that of increasing numbers of wounded people waiting to become healers.

The way this book has turned out, with sections not in logical order–but hopefully standalone–and repetition where someone's story dovetails into another person's tale, it may seem like a pack of cards that has been shuffled. Any chronology of sequences from Ace through the numerals to Jack, King, Queen has certainly been lost, but who would start a game without a pack that has been shuffled?

Though this randomness is partly due to my asperger's, I like to think that it is also influenced by cosmic serendipity. The end in sight, it seems time to share a chronological sequence of encounters that show how meeting one wounded healer can not only lead you to others who are wounded but reveal the identities of those doing the wounding.

'Michael' was a young man with learning difficulties who used to meet up with our outreach teams in the mid-1980s. He wasn't homeless, but he needed non-judgemental company and an occasional brew.

We often met with groups of those we were working with in cafés around the city centre. There were two such establishments near Piccadilly bus station, in the façade of Sunley Buildings, or Piccadilly Plaza as it was known in the day. One was called the Milk Maid; I can't recall the other. Piccadilly Radio had its studios above, on the upper floors of the plaza.

These were large establishments with a busy footfall of shoppers, workers and travellers by bus and train, for they were close to the Manchester transport hubs of the day.

One afternoon, when entering one of these cafés, a homeless man was assisting a blind volunteer to the table while I queued to order for about a dozen volunteers and homeless folk.

As the long queue moved slowly towards the busy till, Michael and one of the volunteers came over to tell me that one of the homeless guys was being asked to leave as he had been seen sleeping rough in the café doorway when the duty manager opened up that morning.

I'd just placed an order for drinks and sandwiches, which had been totted up at the till, and on hearing this I looked over to where a holier-than-thou type of duty manager was getting all authoritative with our group. My then undiagnosed Aspie nerve was touched and, apologising to the staff that my order was no longer required, I turned to address the crowded café.

"Sorry to disturb you, folks", I began. "But we Lifeshare volunteers have come in here today with friends who are homeless and who want to sit quietly with a brew and chat with those who can help them sort their issues out. The manager over there is asking one of our friends, who happens to have served with the British Army, to leave because he is annoyed to have found him sleeping rough in the café foyer when he opened up today. As our friend can't stay, neither can we, so we are going to the café further along. If any of you believe we should treat homeless people with understanding and kindness, you are more than welcome to join us."

Over half the trays in the queue were clattered down and left on the counter piled with food and drink as, to a round of applause, we moved to the other café further along, followed by more than a score of the previous cafes' customers.

In the new location, we were served without incident, and though people respectfully left us to chat privately, we got many "well done" pats on our shoulders and quiet goodbyes as other customers finished their brews and left, dropping wrapped parcels of food for our friends to enjoy later in the day. Later, someone wrote to the *Manchester Evening News* about the incident and spread the word as to which of the two businesses had shown kindness. Oddly enough, the one that had wished our friend to leave closed down within a couple of months.

As evening approached and having seen us stand up for someone who was being treated as unworthy, Michael opened up. Being so young, one of the volunteers and I had peeled off to walk with him to catch his bus, for we knew the city centre was plagued with paedophiles, pimps and pushers who preyed on vulnerable people.

Chatting with him, we learned that Michael lived in a children's home somewhere along the A6 and that he was very unhappy there due to bullying by staff. He also hinted at other layers of abuse. We didn't probe for exact details, as this could put him off speaking.

Just as his bus came into view, I told him: "You don't have to go back, Michael", and as the line of people at the bus stop got aboard, we told him about the safe house network run in partnership between outreach projects like ours and the Children's Society, with full support from social services and the police.

Michael, I noticed, looked scared when I mentioned social services, but relaxed when I casually made a distinction between different local authorities. He reached his decision and allowed us to make a couple of phone calls that led to his stepping onto a new path through life. That's another story, but it had a better ending than the story he had been in.

Sometime afterwards, with Lifeshare now a registered charity in its own premises and soon to be employing paid workers, volunteers got together for a chat. It was 'Oggy' who suggested we might seek paid work in roles where our insights could prove useful. What we had learned about trauma, he suggested; and about sexual politics and other disadvantages as we'd helped men demobbed at the end of the Second World War find homes and even start their own businesses after years of rough sleeping, or while empowering women with self-confidence and belief or helping homeless people settle into new homes and communities, gave us insights that could be applied to reduce people in at-risk groups becoming homelessness or being sexually exploited in the first place. This proactive approach made sense.

It was a no-brainer! We needed work and we were skilled up for work that could help stop others from falling off the edge. As Oggy specialised in Welfare Rights, he knew where he would be going. Others became probation, police or prison officers. Some of our women helped develop safe house networks for prostitutes and other trafficked people. We agreed to stay in touch so we could call on one another's areas of expertise.

My role as a war generation padre, for example, enabled us to access the skills of resistance fighters who'd got Jewish Children and British airmen to safety under the radar of the hostile Nazi regime. Their skills helped us develop anti-trafficking strategies.

Imagine how useful that would become during international sporting events, when thousands of women and girls are trafficked by criminal gangs who know that many men away from home have more money than conscience. Years later, I was headhunted by the police as an adviser, and when I met the senior officer who had invited me to consider the role, was pleased to see a Lifeshare volunteer who, as a young student, had once sat with me through a long night waiting for a train that would take two runaway children to safety. Back then, he had been uncertain about what he would do in life. This city can be grateful he made the choice he did.

To earn a salary, I applied to work with children preparing to leave the care system and got a job as a residential social worker in an independence unit. Lifeshare was still waiting to get salaries to employ paid workers, so for a while longer I remained in my role of founding director to see it through. When that decision saw me caught up in the Strangeways riots as a negotiator, my director of social services came to see me at the Strangeways Crisis Centre. On realising that many of the prisoners were kids on remand and some of them were kids our authority had parental responsibility for, he told me to stay with it. My line manager did not agree. The Bishop of Manchester and Tony Lloyd MP both rang her to explain that my skills were needed at the prison just now. I'm told her response was: "I don't care if the Queen of England rings me, I want him here!"

She changed her tune, however, when a call came from Buckingham Palace. Thanks, Lizzy. It was an honour to serve on your watch.

The riots over, I returned to work. A few days later, was assigned to meet a fifteen-year-old girl at a children's home.

My role was to help her make the transition from the care home she was in, to our unit, so we could prepare her for independent living in the next few years. I'd never seen the children's home, but as I crossed the A6 on my approach, I spotted the bus that Michael had used to get home after meeting us in Manchester, and suddenly realised I may be going to the place where he had been so unhappy.

The manager was out when I arrived but one of the staff led me to a sitting room to wait for the teenager. There was something in the dynamic between staff and young people that had my hackles rising, but while I was working out what it was that was crossing my Aspie empathy radar, a very slender young girl came in and began to address me with the rapidity of a Bren Gun. Her body language and the animated way she talked about her "good friend" the manager made it clear almost immediately that the girl I'd been asked to meet had been groomed by and was being abused by the manager of whom she spoke. She seemed to think him the best thing since sliced bread.

When in due course the manager arrived, he looked down his nose at me as a small cog in the mighty engine he controlled. Little did he realise he was exposing his dark secrets to an empath Aspie, whose own experiences as a kid in care had been honed by Lifeshare insights. My worst fears were confirmed: I was in the presence of a predatory abuser.

When I shared my suspicions with my line manager, an investigation was set in motion. Her abuser was suspended from his job; the girl I was supposed to help now hated me with a vengeance. She blamed me for pulling the rug from under her feet and destroying the only reality she had known.

With her abuser facing an investigation that may lead to charges, it was no longer possible for the girl to come to us, as I would be called to give evidence when things came to a head. Instead, she went to live in an all-female survivors' project, where they could help her dismantle the false reality her abuser had been defining for her and deal with the harm his actions had done to her at so many levels.

One evening after the hearing had been done and dusted, I was working at the independence unit when the phone rang.

"David?" A woman enquired. "There's someone here who'd like to speak to you".

The next voice I heard was a far calmer fifteen-year-old Lisbeth–I'll call her that, as the character *Lisbeth Salander* in Stieg Larsson's *Millennium* series comes to mind whenever I think about her.

"Hello Dave", she began.

I waited.

"I'm sorry", she said. "I was so mean to you, but now I know you were helping me…"

"You've nothing to be sorry for", I assured her. "Though I acted for your own good, my actions brought sudden changes to your life. I couldn't expect you to react any other way than you did, so I've not taken it personally. Lisbeth, I'm just pleased you are getting stronger now. I wish you well. Please just get back on your journey and be the wonderful person I'm sure you are."

In time, Lisbeth did come to our independence unit. She requested me for her keyworker.

As the Children Act many of our Lifeshare network partners had been supporting through parliament came into being, I was among the first Aftercare Social Workers appointed in the country. Lisbeth was among the young people I supported into further education and helped find somewhere to live. Sometime afterwards, I was working out of an office in the now decommissioned children's home where Lisbeth, Michael before her and many others had been so unhappy, when the phone rang.

"Dave!" It was Lisbeth. "How you doing, Magic-Man?" She had got to calling me this after I joined the Magic Circle and started using magic to explain empowering things to young people. She told me she was suing the local authority, as she now knew that two other social workers and an educational psychologist had tried to expose her abuser before I had but had been ignored. She was fuming that the local authority had known something may be going on, but chose to leave her in that situation. Their lawyers were saying her evidence was unsafe due to her mental health.

"Dave, what can I do?"

"Get your solicitor to subpoena me."

She took my advice, which opened yet another can of worms. It wasn't easy for me but was far less so for her. After another gruelling ordeal, she was at last heard, believed and awarded compensation. We both knew that being heard and believed was far more important than the compensation.

Time went by and I was the community coordinator for the team raising funds to rebuild Gorton Monastery. Audrey and I were managing the Angels, a hub for community development.

We had created The Angels in a vacated school and were working away happily one day when Audrey told me there was a call for me.

"Hello, David here."

"Hi, Magic-Man!" It was Lisbeth. She told me she had something she wanted to give me and how she'd tried to contact me through social services and been gutted to learn I no longer worked there.

"Then I saw this TV program about the monastery and there you were. Can I come and see you?"

We agreed to meet in our café for coffee. Audrey agreed to be present, as I was a little worried Lisbeth wanted to give me some of her compensation money, which she'd tried to do on a previous occasion.

When Lisbeth came, she was accompanied by another young woman whom I'd also worked with and whom I'd encouraged to write to help her ventilate at a time when she was trapped by unhappy circumstances. I introduced them to Audrey, and we got comfy around a table with brews.

"You may not know, but we two were friends when we were in the care system", Lisbeth explained. "We were always trying to help each other and one day we were chatting when we realised that we both knew you, Magic-Man. We thought it would be nice to do something to show you we had not forgotten how you believed in us and took risks to help us."

Out of the corner of my eye, I could see Audrey smiling.

"That was a few years ago", the other woman was saying. I could tell Audrey had guessed a little of where this was going. "Anyway, we have each brought you something to show you that you were right, and we both had far brighter futures than others were predicting for us or were even actively denying us."

"You know I can't accept anything…"

"Too late, we've already given it whether you want to accept or not."

"Listen to them", Audrey said with a chuckle.

"Right, here you go." Reaching into their bags, each woman plonked something heavy on the table that astonished me. They were smiling huge grins of pride. Audrey was grinning too.

"Well done, the pair of you!" she said with feeling.

Plonking myself back down, I think I may have cried with pride at their astonishing achievements. On the table before us were two folders containing their coursework, dissertations and university degrees. They had both trained and qualified as social workers.

"You, Mr Magic Man!", Lisbeth said, waving a finger at me and with a twinkle in her eyes, "are not the only one who, having been in care as a child, can go back into a toxic system to make a difference. Me and San are going to make a difference too!"

By Christ, they did! When they introduced me to one of the women who had mentored them, she and I realised our scars had originated in the same narrative. We went on to do a little work together.

Who that mentor was is her story to tell, or not, so I will say no more than what we did together helped young people in our community who were then struggling with overwhelming issues.

Lisbeth and I have stayed in touch and recently she invited me to conduct the funeral of a very close member of her family. Having read this, she agrees it should be out there. We both know the 'our little secret spell' that enables abusers to keep their victims quiet while they continue to wreak havoc. It's not a game either of us wishes to play. Like many of the young people I've had the honour of knowing when they were going through unspeakable battles.

Lisbeth is someone who gives me hope for the future. She calls me the "father of her heart" and she is truly a daughter of my own heart. This outline of her story hardly touches on the courage with which she has fought back from one of the darkest places a human being can find themselves. Not only did she deal with the dragon that was threatening to devour her, but she has also gone on to identify other dragons and slew their ability to bring misery into other people's lives.

The Sharpeville Six

Lifeshare had been running for nine months when, in September 1984, violence erupted in the South African township of Sharpeville. When the deputy mayor was murdered, the apartheid regime reacted by arresting six random members of the vast crowd and sentenced them to death under the 'common purpose' doctrine.

An outraged world began a "Save the Sharpeville Six" campaign.

Contacting Amnesty International, I ran an idea by them. They said it might just work. The next day, I rang the South African embassy in London and had a conversation with their ambassador.

"Listen, my friend, I have a common purpose with that crowd that reacted to an unjust regime that treats some South African citizens as less worthy than others. The murder was terrible, but you plan to hang the wrong people. Can you tell me when it is convenient for me to come and be taken into your custody to hang with these people with whom most of the world has a common purpose?"

The man was clearly upset. I didn't understand. His government was… "civilised".

When the *Manchester Evening News* ran the story of a local dad ready to hang alongside the Sharpeville Six, it started a chain reaction. Those old enough to remember the role Kirk Douglas made famous in the 1960 film might call it the *Spartacus* effect. Across the world, men women and even children started to approach their nearest South African embassy or consulate asking to be taken into custody to share the fate of the Sharpeville Six.

Perhaps the apartheid regime didn't have enough rope, because in the end the Sharpeville Six did not hang and, within a symbolic six years, President F. W. de Klerk was negotiating the end of apartheid. In 1990, apartheid opponent Nelson Mandela was released from prison too, in due course, become president of the new–to use Bishop Desmond Tutu's phrase–'Rainbow Nation' of South Africa.

Much can change over a lifetime. Many believed South Africa would always be run by a racist regime; while few thought that the Berlin Wall would come down in the twentieth century. These things reflect the spiritual walls that are falling all across the world as people wake up to the realisation that human beings are a family that creed, culture and philosophy can't segregate.

In 1984, I had no idea that one day I would meet a white South African police officer who, having worked within the apartheid regime went on to become a bodyguard for Nelson Mandela. But I did and he taught me many things. Nor did I comprehend that when seeking advice from the great Desmond Tutu about Manchester gang conflicts he would write back: "You are the man whom God has given insight in that place. You don't need my advice. Show your community how to stand in its power."

The world isn't static. It can and does change–for the better when ordinary people dare to stand in their power.

PART 3

STORIES FROM THE STREETS

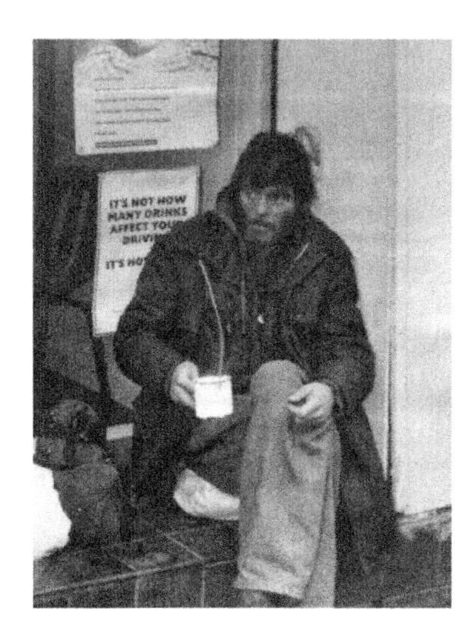

Tony, one of many failed by Thatcher's 'Care in the Community'.

In 1983, realising 'care in the community' was leading to people with mental health problems sleeping rough, we invited Manchester University to help us organise a rough sleepers census. It came as little surprise to discover that some 200 people slept rough in the city centre on an average night. The following year, we launched Lifeshare so we could begin to address their needs.

Enough time has now gone by to share the stories of some of those we encountered during those early years without revealing their identities. Real names will not be used.

'Arthur'

Arthur was lying on a urine-saturated mattress in a derelict railway arch when we found him. Unable to move due to tuberculosis, pneumonia and other serious health problems, he was drinking the dubious trickles that festooned the walls. His body was a mess of rat and flea bites, but he refused all offers of help. I arranged for myself and a couple of volunteers to visit him daily. We made a point of eating our lunch with him, though it was two days before he'd accept so much as a drink of orange, three days before we had the conversation that changed his life.

"We appreciate that, living like this, you say you wish to die, Arthur. We are not here to override your personal decisions, though we would prefer that you made such a momentous one from a position of health."

"I'm going to no hospital. I'd stand out like a sore thumb with no visitors."

Taking a deep breath, I made a promise I didn't know I could keep.

"You will be visited every day and once you're well, if you still wish to come back here and die, I'll come with you and sit beside you until you do."

Arthur chose to get medical help, but when it came, the ambulance crew refused to cross the croft into the squalor of the railway arch. When I lifted him to carry Arthur to the ambulance, this six-foot man, who was emaciated, came up in my arms like a toddler.

Once Arthur was settled on a ward at Salford Royal Hospital, I did a ring round to get a rota of volunteers who would visit him every day. Among those visitors was the young son of one of our volunteers, who called in on his way home from school. He seemed to remind Arthur of his own son and the two struck up a bond that led to Arthur agreeing we could trace his family.

Interestingly his sister, who had lost touch with Arthur when she was young, had become a social worker who helped people while they were in hospital. She helped us to piece together his story.

Discharged from the army, Arthur had gotten depressed and just wandered off one day. For twenty years he had lived in hostels or on the streets. Wherever he went, people saw an alcoholic. We now knew something very different was going on, and persuaded the hospital to do a psychiatric assessment while they were healing his many physical wounds.

"He's a typical alcoholic", one doctor told me haughtily.

"Really? He's been here a fortnight. Has he shown any signs of delirium tremens?"

That reached him, and the doctor's certainty deflated as he knew he'd simply allowed himself to associate all homeless people with alcohol addiction.

"You're right. We'll arrange a psychiatric assessment".

Soon, Arthur was being treated for depression. He made remarkable progress once his actual state rather than his supposed state was being addressed. The day came when he was ready to move into the flat we had found for him. Going to collect him from the hospital, I dreaded keeping the possibility that I might have to keep the second part of my promise to him.

Arthur settled into the passenger seat, and we set off to view his flat. Turning a corner, the railway arch in which he had once skippered loomed into view. On impulse, I stopped the car and we both sat there very quietly.

"Well?" I asked at last.

"You bugger!" Arthur grinned. "You were right. Seeing my sister again and being as well as I've been since I was in the army, I've something to live for now. I'm meeting my son next week. Not seen him since he was a toddler. Best go and get that flat ship shape so he has somewhere to meet his dad."

Many can be grateful that Arthur decided to live. Not long afterwards, he went through the Lifeshare training and became a volunteer. Even the people he had skippered with didn't recognise the smart, clean-shaven man who handed them soup and good advice. All they felt was his empathy and kindness.

Within a year of getting a place to live, Arthur had been to college and was ready to start his own business. The last time I saw him, many years ago, he had four employees, one of whom had also become homeless after leaving the forces.

When a machine breaks, we repair it. When a human being breaks… well, there are plenty more where that one came from. Arthur is living proof that no human being can be written off and that by practising our humanity, all our lives can be made a little richer.

The Bishop with Strangeways

In Easter 1990, as director of Lifeshare, it fell to me to set up a crisis centre and bring together a negotiating team when there was a riot at

Strangeways Prison, now HMP Manchester.

Caterers, counsellors, healers, faith-leaders and a wide variety of compassionate people I had met over the years responded to my call for help, among them Stanley Booth Clibborn, who was at that time Bishop of Manchester. Within a couple of hours of my ringing him to say we needed a building close to the prison, 'Stan the Man' as he was affectionately known, had identified a church close enough to fit the bill and by day two we had set up a place where prison officers and prisoners' families could come for refreshments and to gain news of their loved ones caught up in a situation.

Stan would come down in ordinary clothes and help out in the centre.

"Who's that nice chap washing up and making everyone a brew", a visiting Liverpool gang member asked one day while we were chatting about finding his brother in the prison system. "That's the Bishop of Manchester, mate".

"The chuff it is! Who is it really?"

Even then, most people saw the church as out of touch and only interested in converting people, but Stan broke the mould. He was one of the best examples I ever had of someone who put what they preached into practice and was instrumental in my becoming a Franciscan after the riots, eventually nudging me towards priesthood.

As well as providing the building and mucking in, when he learned that I and the rest of the negotiating team only caught a maximum four hours of sleep in short snatches each day, Stan opened his home to myself and team members so that when we did snatch our ration of sleep, at least it was away from the distractions of the centre in the comfort of the beds at Bishopscourt. We were woken on cue with a fresh brew before being driven back to continue the work of bringing a peaceful solution for all caught up in a difficult situation.

1990 Strangeways Prison riot, when the author was a negotiator.

With rumours of deaths that later proved unfounded, police officers, members of prisoners' families and prison officers alike were tense in their mutual anxiety. Not all prisoners, even those shipped out to other prisons, were accounted for in the role calls that were being updated on the go. They were not all tough old lags inside that prison, either. Many were kids on remand who had not been found guilty of anything and were extremely vulnerable. So, when a certain 'nudes-paper', that I will not give air to by naming it, ran a front-page poll asking readers to vote on whether the SAS should go in, I was furious.

The press had been doing all in its power to find the crisis centre, but Stan's press officer, chaplain and legal advisers were active in ensuring our location wasn't compromised. In my fury at that poll, I rang the paper in question. So convinced were they that I had decided to accept a fee to tell our story, they put me through to the editor.

"You slime-ball!" I screamed at him down the phone, "You will not even get this story after the event for causing so much human misery and using a decent British regiment as your pawn!" After telling him to do something biologically impossible, I slammed the phone down and turned around to see the kind, gentle soul I had come to respect standing before me with an envelope.

"The chaplains have had a whip round for your work here", said the bishop, handing me the envelope with a twinkle in his eyes. "David, can I ask? Who were you just talking to?"

Feeling ashamed to have uttered such harsh words in this good man's hearing, I told him. On learning it had been the editor of the newspaper in question, the bishop responded: "Was it really!" He then dipped into his wallet to add another £20 to the fund, before adding an enthusiastic: "Well done!"

That was Stan. When I think of him, I think of Jesus in his angrier moments such as cleansing the temple or calling Herod a Fox, which I suspect is the ancient Hebrew equivalent of 'slime-ball'. He was a good man who saw the innate goodness in others.

Stan used his position to get things done in my home city. Perhaps when I've worked out the difference between the official secrets act thirty-year statute of limitations and freedom of information, I might share just how much that wonderful man, now gone to his heavenly reward, put himself out to stop Manchester from falling into violent anarchy at a point when vultures were gathering to tear our society apart. You will just have to wait and see on that count.

One thing I can relate to is how, when the siege was over, Stan stepped in to cut Thatcher's Home Office bods off at the pass. He walked in on them telling me and the team we were now privy to sensitive information and could not go home until we'd agreed to a debrief with their intelligence officers. As it was thanks to their incompetence that the siege had gone on for the best part of a month when it would have been over on day three had they not interfered in our negotiations, I was digging my heels in and getting my coat on.

"Gentlemen", Stan said disarmingly to the ministry bods. "As a bishop who sits in the House of Lords, I'm sure you won't mind if I offer myself as their debriefing officer".

Before they could pick their chins up off the floor, Stan was ushering us outside and marching us towards his chauffeur and up the road towards Bishopscourt.

"Just keep going", he advised. "They'll probably follow us, but they won't dare cross my threshold. We'll have a brew and some toast by way of that 'debrief' and when they've lost interest, simply make your way back home to your families."

His ploy worked and got the arrogant, entitled numpties off our backs.

Stan knew that I'd got to Silver Control at the start of the riots by looking for an alley guarded by a policeman, showing him my library card, which announced me as D. C. Gray and boldly knocking on the door of the operations caravan. Though the officer who opened the door tried to fob me off, his superior recognised my voice from a previous occasion when I'd talked a vulnerable man off the roof of a department store.

"That's David Gray. Take him to meet the overview team, he'll be useful in this situation."

The others had all gone home, and Stan and I were about to say goodnight when he asked: "David, tell me why you spent a month away from your family getting little sleep and lying in the debris of a prison talking to strangers who may not have treated you kindly."

"The God I know would have sent someone to help me find my way down from that roof had it been me up there."

"That's a very priestly insight", said Stan. "You'd make a fine priest."

"Not sure I would", I replied. "I've too many rough edges. Besides, I'm quite comfortable where Jesus was, on the streets among the poor, the marginalised, the despised, the homeless and those in need of love and affirmation of their personhood."

"But you will be visiting the lads in the various prisons they will be sent to. Look, do me a favour", he rummaged in a draw and produced a clip-on dog collar "When you visit, do so as a friend of the family or as the social worker you are in your professional life. But will you also make a few visits wearing this, then come back to tell me what happened?"

Wanting to go home, I took the collar and left. It was so good to see Elaine and the family again.

Over the next few weeks, I did indeed make several visits to prisoners who had been caught up in the riots. When I went as a family friend through Partners of Prisoners support, I'd be asked to leave all my belongings in a locker in the visitor's centre and, having been searched, join a queue, taking only the key to the locker into the prison with me. When I went as a social worker, my case was examined and I'd join a shorter queue, before having a private consultation with the prisoner I was visiting.

One day, after driving for several hours, I arrived at a prison I'd never visited before.

Remembering my promise to Stan, I reached into the glove compartment for the dog-collar, which I placed around my neck.

"Hello", I said at the gate. "I've come to see prisoner number..."

"He's on garden duties today. Go through that gate, up the hill beyond and through the next gate and you'll find them having a brew about now."

The gates he indicated were heavy-duty, high-security prison gates.

"How do I get through those gates?" I had asked.

"Sorry", said the guard, handing me his keys. "Drop these back here as you're leaving."

When I reported this to Stan, he agreed with me that it was wrong that a piece of plastic gave a person privilege and trusts they ought to enjoy naturally in an honest exchange between people.

"You are right, of course", he admitted. "We both know clergy, police officers and others who abuse their powers and position, but the fact is being a priest will open doors for you to help people who need that Jesus of the marginalised you know so well."

Seven years after the riots and another bishop down the line, I was ordained. It was the first time that Rabbi and Krishna devotees were present to affirm the calling of a priest at Manchester's Anglican Cathedral. I went on to do further training with One Spirit Interfaith Faculty, which has its roots in a meeting at the end of the Second World War, in which priests, imams, rabbis and humanists discussed how they could work together for a kinder world.

Then, thirteen years into my Anglican ministry and yet another bishop later, the previously mentioned Reverend Mike Williams, whom I'd known since the late 1970s and under whom I'd served as a perpetual, voluntary curate, retired. Now Franciscan and Interfaith advisor to the present bishop, when a man who disliked children, looked down on women and expressed racist opinions came to replace Mike in the three parishes Mike had served lovingly, which lay in a community where I'd helped restore a Franciscan monastery to inspire and empower local people, I went to see the serving bishop. Entering Bishopscourt, where I'd slept as the guest of one of his predecessors, it was clear that the energy had changed since Stan had been in charge of things here.

"Bishop, you can't put a man like that in charge of parishes where decent people of all faiths and none cooperate and respect each other", I told him.

"You need to understand, David", he had replied haughtily, "That man has employment rights, while you do not".

"You will be aware that I've been active tidying up the mess in organised religion and elsewhere and looking after the victims of appalling abuse."

The bishop nodded.

"You will also be aware that I have a learning difficulty."

Again, he indicated his awareness.

"May I ask you, bishop, do you know the difference between Asperger's and Tourette's?"

"Not sure I do, David", he admitted.

"Then you can fuck off!" I replied as, in deep disappointment and with much pain, I turned my back on organised religion.

Not long afterwards, I received a call from the leadership council of the Progressive Christian Alliance who, having heard that I stood by my principles and left the church better to follow Jesus, invited me to accept the role of a servant leader to Britain and the Island to help build a network of people who have a proven record of ministering to their communities while serving people of all faiths and none without prejudice or favour. My world and ministry were about to change dramatically.

While a servile chaplain in the Royal Air Force wing decided that, now I wasn't under a bishop's license, I was no longer eligible to be an Air Cadet chaplain, the veterans' networks–who knew me well–held firm. Too, prison governors were awakening to the fact that the 'Jesus is the answer' type approach only worked to keep most prisoners on the straight and narrow up to the point where they walked through the gates at the end of their sentences, while the approaches of progressive Interfaith, Humanist and Pagan ministers that engaged with offenders as who they are, light and dark, was having a more lasting impact that was helping reduce recidivism. The path that Stan set me upon has enabled me to affirm bikers, outreach workers, homeless people, LGBT+ folk, people who've been through mental health services, serving prisoners and others as ministers through our refreshing ministry scheme of wounded healers.

At times, I imagine Stan, who died in 1996, quietly observing what I'm up to and chuckling to himself. Like Saint Francis before him, Stan knew that every Saint has a past, and every Sinner has a future.

Where the Luftwaffe Failed

It has been said that people don't need government so much as governments need people. In a crazy world where those we elected are closing down services that support the most vulnerable–and we are all vulnerable at some stages of life–the arrogance of those with power is like a stab to the heart of our national life. As our libraries, swimming baths, school building and health provision come under attack, I'm reminded of the Second World War veteran who sighed as he watched his community destroyed in the slum clearances, "They are doing to us what the Luftwaffe failed to achieve."

A fellow radio presenter sent me this recently:

> After Germany invaded Poland in September 1939, many places of learning and culture–universities, schools, libraries, museums, theatres and cinemas, were closed or designated 'Nur für Deutsche' (Germans Only). Twenty-five museums and a host of other institutions were destroyed during the war. One estimate indicates: by the war's end 43% of the infrastructure of Poland's educational-research institutions and 14% of its museums had been destroyed. Just 105 of pre-war Poland's 175 museums survived the war. Only 33 of these institutions were able to reopen. Of pre-war Poland's 603 scientific institutions, half were totally destroyed. Few survived the war relatively intact.

Are we allowing today's politicians to do to our communities what the Luftwaffe failed to achieve? But it got worse. That piece of internet research continues:

> Many university professors, teachers, lawyers, artists, writers, priests and other members of the Polish intelligentsia were arrested and executed, or transported to concentration camps… During World War II Poland lost 39-45% of its physicians and dentists.
>
> Poland also lost 26-57% of its lawyers, 15-30% of its teachers, 30-40% of its scientists and university professors, and 18-28% of its clergy. The Jewish intelligentsia was exterminated altogether. The reasoning behind this policy was articulated by one Nazi gauleiter, who said: "In my district, any Pole who shows signs of intelligence will be shot."

The current climate of public apathy and government arrogance allows a far-right party to spread rumours and lies aimed at dividing Britain against itself while its members list British citizens they propose to kill. How much fear and misery are they creating in the name of an all-white Britain of mediocrity that would again pull the world into chaos?

Should we worry? No! Prepare? Yes! I believe in Britain, and I believe that the majority of British people will stand up and pull together.

Perhaps for the good of all we should, perhaps, be offering therapy to the damaged people who need scapegoats for their inadequacies, but we can never submit to them. Britain has a proud tradition of standing up to bullies and tyrants at home and abroad.

A Very Good Friday

A few years ago, when Gorton was still the most disadvantaged community in Western Europe, older people who could remember the golden age when it had been the workshop of the world wondered if the good times would ever return.

One old lady, Elizabeth, used to talk about when there were jobs for all and the factories had brass bands, while local churches had choirs - not the 'karaoke' tape machines we were now obliged to use.

Elizabeth took ill. When she finally settled into a local care home, I went to see her.

"What's going on in the world, David?" she'd asked.

"Well, Elizabeth, there's now a community art group; we will be holding festivals again soon and we've just started a community choir. On Good Friday, they will be singing at my church service."

"Och, David", she said, with a big tear in her eye, "Sure, I'll never hear them!"

On Good Friday during the service, I mentioned Elizabeth and what she had said, adding that if anyone wished to prove her wrong, they should meet me in the car park. When I got outside, all sixteen members of the choir were waiting. Luckily, I'd known matron from childhood, and she didn't bat an eyelid when I turned up with so many visitors for Elizabeth. Not being one to cross a threshold without an invitation, I went in first so as not to overwhelm her.

"Elizabeth, I've a few folk who'd like to meet you. Would you mind?"

"Not at all", she'd responded, "help me sit up in bed first will you."

As the choir members filed in and began to surround her bed, there were gasps of recognition.

"O, hello! I think I used to see you shopping on Gorton Market!"

"Aren't you the lady who lived near the allotments?"

"That's me, but who are you?"

"This, Elizabeth, is that choir I was telling you about. The one you said you'd never hear. They wanted to prove you wrong, especially as you have done so much to keep the community going, they thought you should hear its new voice..."

As we sang *May the Lord Send Angels*, Elizabeth was visibly lifted before our eyes to a new sense that heaven had not, after all, abandoned the community she had loved so long.

She seemed to rise up in her bed in rapture as she understood that all her hopes had not been in vain.

Elizabeth died shortly afterwards. The choir that helped bring her a deepening of that peace she had known in life went on to sing at festivals, in prisons, at cathedrals, mosques and concert venues touching many with the voice of a community that had learned to sing itself into a healthier state of being.

Pulpit Misdirection

Some years ago, Malcolm Solomons of North Manchester was a proud member of a brass band. The only Jewish member of that band, he was happy to accompany them to play at all sorts of events, including Christian festivals.

One Whit Week in the High Peak, the band was playing hymns for an annual church event Malcolm had taken part in for several years. In a village square nearby the church, the minister began to preach.

Malcolm and his Christian friends could not believe their ears. The man was using scripture to suggest that the Jewish people were solely responsible for the execution of Jesus. The whole band felt deflated as they walked away at the end of the service.

Malcolm took up the issue with the local bishop and in due course, a meeting was arranged with the priest concerned. The man was mortified. He had genuinely had no idea that his take on scripture at that time could be so hurtful and offered an unconditional apology, which Malcolm was pleased to accept.

When I heard the story at a Holocaust Memorial event, it had me wondering how often harmful and misleading interpretations of sacred writings still occur. Even today when we know that the inspired word of God in the Bible, Koran and other scriptures becomes flawed in the translation by men with ways of seeing the world that can never come close to God's view, there are those who leap at passages they take out of context to justify their deeply held fears, prejudices and insecurities. Such people will justify the subjugation of women, the castigation of children, racism, homophobia and slavery in the shadow cast by the light of scripture.

Sadly, in the name of church unity or faith solidarity, many good folk who sat meditatively with scripture and opened their hearts to the enlightening spirit allowed the seeds of inquisition, Holocaust and burning times to fester underground to erupt as the weeds that would sap the air and nutrient from the good crop that humanity needs to produce if it is to end the blights of injustice, prejudice, greed and power-lust that resurface time and again to withhold the promise of global justice just beyond our reach. Faith unity can never be at the expense of the light itself.

As Malcolm's story shows, when good people are bold enough to constructively challenge, other good people are enabled to ponder anew perhaps long-held misunderstandings and bring them into the clean air and light. In so doing they move us nearer to a time when people will be respected for their identity, lovingly challenged in their errors and free to fall in love in a world where resources are shared, and all are willing to labour for the good of themselves and their neighbours. The real danger is that no one dares challenge, and the downward spiral continues in its ignorance.

The Senior Service

This comes from a time when a senior Manchester police officer was promoting a judgemental approach to policing in the name of the Christian God.

After a hotel meeting with high-powered folk who'd agreed to help raise awareness around homelessness and child prostitution; I and a successful young woman in her late twenties remained to finalise arrangements.

Ordering more coffee, we sat in companionable silence completing our notes.

"Do you know", I observed, breaking the silence, "I've never met a prostitute who hadn't been abused as a child nor folk with big hearts who haven't suffered."

Looking at me across the table, some new quality took rest within her eyes as if she was trying to reach a decision. She began hesitantly, but as her story unfolded, I marvelled at her courage, at the dignity of those of whom she spoke. Soon, I found my own eyes moist, and my heart humbled.

She had been fourteen when her father started to abuse her. When she was sixteen, she noticed that his attentions were being drawn to her younger sister who was the age she had been when he had betrayed her trust and innocence. After a heart-to-heart, the two girls decided to flee.

Like many escaping domestic violence, they fled on the spur of the moment with little preparation.

That night, the girls found themselves in an all-night café. Realising their money was almost spent; the older girl reached a tough decision.

"Wait here. I won't be long."

Leaving her sister in the café, she walked around the corner. Men, she knew, sometimes paid for what her father had taken. Standing terrified, she was approached by an older woman.

"What you doing here, sweetheart?"

"I don't know why", my friend told me. "But I burst into tears and told her everything."

"You go back to your sister", the woman had told her handing her a fiver. "Wait in that café and I'll come and collect you when we've done."

Trustingly, she had returned. Over an hour later, the woman, in company with two other women, came for them.

"You are staying with us tonight", they had stated.

Desperate for somewhere warm to sleep, the sisters had gone with them. The house was shared by several women. A few weeks later when her sister was safe in her new school, my friend wanted to thank the women who had looked so kindly on two strangers.

"All we women here were abused as children and now we make our living as prostitutes. But you and your sister, sweetheart, are going to avoid the trap and live the lives we should have lived."

Given the best education, both girls went on to happy and successful lifestyles. My friend swore me to secrecy.

"My sister never knew how the women who gave us a safe home and acted like mothers to us earned their living", she explained. "If you will keep my story under wraps, one day I'll let you know when it's time for it to be told."

The years went by, and we lost touch. Then, one day, out of the blue, I got a phone call.

"The woman I met that night, when I was sixteen and my sister was just fourteen, has died. I've told my sister everything now, though to be honest she guessed most of it. I've been sort of following your career and have discussed it with my sister–will you do the funeral? My sister and I and one of the women who shared that house agree it's time the story was told, and we'd like you to tell it as part of her eulogy."

That was a very powerful funeral at many levels.

There are still many who judge the women of the senior service. I hope that perhaps the sharing of this tale will mean there are now fewer inclined to do so.

The Baby and the Harlot

'Cagney' and 'Lacey' were talking with a young prostitute, 'Julie', as I drove the soup-run van north to drop off a volunteer who had to be up for work the next day.

"Listen, you lot", I said, "I'm falling asleep and need a coffee. Do you mind if we call at my house before I drop you all back?"

At the time, my youngest son, Richard, was in Booth Hall Hospital. Normally, I visited after the soup-run, but with Julie and two others to drop off, it would be midnight before I could be there, so I rang to let the staff know.

"Don't be daft", they said, "Come on your way and bring the team with you." So, refreshed by the coffee, the four of us set off. What happened next changed Julie's life.

"Hello, Boychick! You need changing!" I greeted Richard.

Having changed my profoundly handicapped infant son's clothing, I handed him to the nearest person, to free me up to deal with his bed sheets. Moments later, Richard was chuckling away while Julie had begun sobbing inconsolably.

When I turned, Julie was holding Richard. As they gazed into each other's eyes, Cagney and Lacey stood on either side holding the scene.

As we dropped her off, Julie told us she couldn't believe I'd handed my beloved son to a whore with a heroin habit. Her son was on another Booth Hall ward. She was allowed nowhere near him. Some weeks later I got a call from a psychiatrist at Prestwich Hospital.

"What did you do to Julie?"

"Pardon?"

"Sorry", she said, "I'm not accusing you; I'm just amazed that this woman whose life was in chaos has not had a fix since the night she went to Booth Hall with you. She's clean, has left her abusive partner and is working to regain custody of her son. Will you come and speak about Lifeshare to our staff?"

Cagney and Lacey were on shift with me again for some weeks. As we turned the mini-bus into Chorlton Street, our hearts sank as a familiar figure stepped out and flagged us down. It was Julie. Had she ended up back here after all that promise?

"Hi!" She squealed, hugging the women. "I wanted to tell you my news and knew no other way to find you again! My son is coming to live with me next week. I'm clean and I'm staying that way!"

"Good on you, Julie!" said one of her old friends, who was still plying the trade, "If you can do it, there's hope for an old tart like me." All the women laughed. There was hope in their laughter. Julie had stepped into her birthright to be clean. She brought up her boy and they are both rightly proud of each other. Julie still lives in our city, where she works in computers. Her son? Let's just say there's another police officer with valuable insights working to keep Manchester safe for everyone.

The Habit

We discouraged volunteers from wearing uniforms or religious insignia while out meeting the homeless with Lifeshare in the 1980s, having learned that, for many, such things could trigger distress rooted in past traumas. Nuns who did our training and joined the volunteer force were asked to wear normal clothes and let their kindness be their habit.

But there was one elderly nun who I almost didn't put through induction, as 'Sister Kathleen', adamantly refused to wear anything but her habit. One night, we were grateful that she did so.

As well as our outreach to homeless people, we did a 10pm 'Tea-Break' for sex industry workers near the old Chorlton Street Bus Station. Cagney and Lacey, two of our women volunteers, had developed a good relationship with 'Kelly', a prostitute who had a £60 a day heroin habit. Kelly's life was controlled by her violent partner. The policy of a chief constable who ordered that the women be arrested at every opportunity only served to keep them trapped, for a court appearance meant having to come back to work off the fine, giving no space to deal with controlling men or addictions.

One night, Kelly had stepped into the back of our minibus to enjoy a brew and a chat when suddenly, obviously under the impression our team of volunteers were a block booking, 'Gene Hunt' and the team screeched to a halt in front of us and piled out to give us umbrage. Kelly started to tremble. Another fine might scupper Kelly's last hopes of getting clean.

Just as we thought we were in for a lengthy grilling, Sister Kathleen popped her head out of the window and in her sternest, commanding voice shouted: "Halt! Where do you think you boys are going?"

At least one of the startled vice squad officers must have been a good Catholic lad, for they froze in their tracks. "Leave these women alone, they're with me!" Sister Kathleen ordered. The vice squad dutifully turned on their heels and made off.

Kelly, shaking with relief, fell into the arms of the elderly nun and sobbed her heart out.

We headed off to drop the good sisters back at their convent, Kelly in the back with Cagney and Lacey. By the time we returned to drop her off, Kelly had done some ventilating of long-stagnant feelings and had decided as to the future she wanted for herself. Kelly, of course, is not her real name. I'm pleased to say she's out there still, working to help women trapped by the sort of life conditions she knew only too well to explore wider possibilities for their futures.

Policing approaches have changed considerably since Sister Kathleen saw off Gene Hunt. Though they retain all their enforcement powers, Greater Manchester Police officers have other tools in their kit in 21st Century Manchester and are better equipped to signpost people to support that can help them change negative lifestyles and move to the side of the Angels.

Footnote: We hear such horror stories of historic abuses by members of religious orders, but the other side of the story is that there are still those who do genuinely good work. Sister Kathleen's order is among them.

With help and guidance from some of the women who had worked in the resistance networks that helped get Jewish children and allied combatants down the lines to safety under the radar of the Nazi occupation of Europe during the Second World War, two orders of nuns, in particular, played a vital role in helping Lifeshare's women develop the safe house network that still supports women who are trafficked and forced into sexual activity to break away from controlling men.

Not many people realise how many thousands of women and children are groomed, snatched and trafficked to meet the diabolical demands of violent and indifferent men. While there are indeed religious orders that themselves abuse power, there are others who shine their light into the darkness to expose such abuses and combat the organised criminals who wreak so much misery in our world.

Sadly, so often those organised criminals are members of or connected to establishment institutions of church, state and law enforcement. In this twenty-first century, it is surely time we worked with decent politicians, clergy, police officers and others to either win those institutions back from the control of those who misuse them and into the hands of people willing to serve the public, justice and decency; or, if not, abolish them forever.

The Grand Old Men of Boxing

In the 1980s, I worked in a Catholic hostel for homeless men at a time when the names of boxers like Spider Kelly; the Galway Blacksmith (Peter Kane) and a certain Joe-Mac were on the lips of living memory. What few knew outside his immediate circle was that Joe himself, was alive and well and living in the backstreets of Ancoats.

The reverence the men afforded Joe was moving. We'd sit in a group around a bottomless tea urn playing cards while sharing stories of boxing. As the evenings wore on, a silence would descend as men wandered quietly with their memories. After a while, Joe would look around with a beaming smile: “I'm a grand old man", he would say, “I'll never die!”

On this note, people would say their goodnights and go their separate ways until the next gathering. From time to time, I’d accompany Joe to Manchester Royal Infirmary for checks. On one visit following a fall, I was stood near his head as he lay on a stretcher, a porter at his feet. Joe suddenly treated us to one of his beaming smiles: “I'm a grand old man”, he began, “I'll never...”

We never heard the end of that sentence, though I am sure it was heard in eternity, for Joe died in the midst of uttering it.

Anyone who knows the history of Manchester knows that the Scuttlers, gangs who terrified our Victorian ancestors, learned to better channel their energy with the advent of Ardwick, Salford, the Adelphi and other Lads Clubs forming a network of concerned activity across the city, bringing years of competitive harmony. In a politically correct era that followed this somehow was forgotten, allowing a rot to set back in that led to the needless loss of young Mancunian lives.

Our city has again awakened to the need for providing sports and leisure activities on a grand scale. Let's hope and pray that she doesn't fall asleep again once the harmony of energetic, friendly rivalry replaces the hopelessness of frightened kids carrying guns and knives.

Joe represented the grand old men of a bygone age in a world where, though boxing had changed much, the courage and principles behind the sport remained timeless. The grand older men of today still keep the sport going, with respect passed like a baton from one generation to the next. Again, we have boxing clubs being developed by caring Mancunians like Kevin Williams, Bob Rimmer, Ken Dobson and Kaya Dundee. The Mancunian, United Estates of Wythenshawe and other boxing clubs across our city are teaching young men and women courage, skill, respect and confidence. They play a crucial role in keeping them and all of us safe as timeless values are nurtured anew in young Sally-Mancunians of all ages and backgrounds.

So, join me in a toast: “To the grand old men of boxing–in every generation–L’chaim!”

The Evangelist's Pitch

Most Britons who affiliate to no formal religion intuitively cherish the golden rule that runs through the major faiths, which Jesus up as: "love Go(o)d and treat others as you wish to be treated." When people struggle to articulate their longing for deeper meaning in the face of silent or even accusatory institutions, society suffers. Despite sensing worth in the faith communities around them, people can be reluctant to cross thresholds into worlds whose languages and formulas can be bewildering to the uninitiated.

Among those affirming my calling as a priest at my ordination in Manchester Cathedral in 1998 were rabbi and Hindu devotees. My association with Judaism goes back to infancy, but it was not until the 1970s, when George Harrison brought the music of the devotees to a wider audience, that I started attending Manchester's Hindu Temple.

Among the mantras we sang as our dancing got wilder and faster were the number one hits *Hare Krishna* and *Govinda*. Thus, did I hone the crescendo leaps I still do, if less gracefully, when on stage with Goldblade. Punk fans often ask me, "Where did you learn to pogo like that?" My answer often surprises them.

As a teen in the book trade with responsibility for developing Faith and Philosophy sections, I gathered together books from all the great faiths on subjects such as Astral Projection, Tibetan Mysticism, the occult and Yellow Magic, undergoing formation as a Yellow Mage myself. Krishna devotees provided copies of the *Bhagavad-Gita* and other books on Hindu spirituality, and our friendship has continued since.

During the 1990 Manchester prison riots, for example, it was Hindu friends who came to the crisis centre every evening to feed us all a wonderful vegetarian meal.

Later that decade, my relationship with the monks gave me an insight as to why so many people turn their back on organised religion. Emerging from the Manchester hearing of the Stephen Lawrence enquiry where I had given evidence on 1980s policing in Manchester, I bumped into devotees feeding homeless people.

Our dancing to their music attracted a small crowd, who seemed ecstatic to see a Christian priest and Hindu Monks celebrating God together while meeting human needs. Somehow, it revealed something of the truth that we are as connected spiritually as we are by our shared humanity.

One well-dressed man came over to hug us and cry on our shoulders.

People are often seen trying to evangelise the crowd on that Market Street pitch, but the crowd usually moves away quickly.

The message of universal love cannot be detected in dogma, but it can be sensed when people move beyond dogma into an unconditional embrace. The recent emergence of the Manchester 'Queerstianity' youth movement in response to a 'hate evangelist' who has set up on that pitch is a healthy sign that society's spiritual immune system is kicking in as people make a stance for compassion across diversity and seek an end to the spiritual bullying of bigots.

Ripper Victims

Some have wondered why I take time to try and promote empathy between Greater Manchester police officers and the communities they serve to protect. Here's a clue:

Polly Nichols, Annie Chapman, Elizabeth Stride, Catherine Eddowes and Mary Kelly are names not, ironically, as well known as the man who murdered them, though he was never officially identified.

These women were victims of the nineteenth century, Whitechapel murderer who came to be known as 'Jack the Ripper'.

Vera Millward & Jean Jordan

Look at the above women whose faces peer at you. Vera and Jean were brutally murdered here in Manchester by 'Yorkshire Ripper' Peter Sutcliffe. It's very important that society remembers such victims and regards their humanity.

Around the time of Sutcliffe's arrest, I was driving up Rochdale Road in the small hours after the soup-run. Ahead of me, a car stopped to pick up a woman pedestrian. Idling behind the car waiting to turn right at Charlestown Road lights, I saw the passenger door open. The woman tried to get out but was pulled back in. Alarmed, I followed, turning my beam up to take the registration and see if she was ok. Realising he'd been spotted, the driver stopped long enough to throw the woman out of the car before driving off at speed.

As I approached, she cowered terrified behind a bus stop. Luckily, an elderly couple happened along with their dog. The female presence eased her fear. She told us she'd accepted a lift from a man she'd seen in the pub earlier, but he'd turned nasty and produced a knife.

We called the police from the phone box on Victoria Avenue. While awaiting their arrival, the woman suddenly screamed and ran off. Her assailant had driven back. Approaching the car, I had to dive out of the way as he drove straight at me before disappearing again.

When a police officer eventually arrived, there was no sign of the woman. The dog walkers and I began to outline the events we'd witnessed.

"How was she dressed?" The officer asked. We described her and I asked if he wanted to know about the driver.

"What I'm trying to establish", he said, "is was she asking for it?"

"What!?"

"Did she look like a slapper?" He said, in a way that suggested he thought me naïve.

Furiously, I responded, "I suppose if Peter Sutcliffe had only murdered prostitutes, you'd have let him get on with it!"

The next day, I complained to a senior officer, who checked the car reg. In due course a man was arrested in connection with a very serious bogus taxi driver offence, and the misogynist police officer was disciplined.

Manchester Evening News agony aunt Joan Seddon agreed to put a discreet message in her column that only the woman victim would understand. It encouraged her to telephone a counselling service.

She did ring–but to this day I'm brought to tears to think her only concern was that her attacker had not run me down.

I'll never know who she was or how she went on but will never forget her concern for a stranger in the wake of her terrible ordeal. I hope she has enjoyed a happy life since.

When the police do a good job, they warrant our respect. When they can't do the job at all due to their inability to see beyond their prejudices and stereotypes, they should get out of the way of those who know what they are doing.

Footnote: The night Vera was murdered, a woman sleeping in a skipper close to the site was disturbed by a man approaching her sleeping space. Fortunately, two men skippering (sleeping rough) in the same location came back and the man hurried off. That poor woman has often wondered whether the man was Sutcliffe. She is a wonderful woman who sorted her issues, and it was my honour to work with her helping vulnerable people in the last quarter of last century, but it was relatively recently that she felt able to share with me what may have been her close call with a killer. Like that good woman, I wonder how safer the world would be if those overlooked and dismissed were able to get their voices heard.

Two Very Courageous Women

There aren't many women you could say were not courageous in some way, but among the most courageous women I've ever met are Patsy McKie and Sylvia Lancaster. Both have gone through the unimaginable torment of one of their children being murdered.

Patsy's son, Dorrie, was shot dead in 1999, while Sylvia's daughter, Sophie, was murdered in 2007 when she and her boyfriend Rob Maltby were attacked by a gang who astonishingly reacted to their lifestyle choice as Goths.

Patsy took hold of her deep pain at the loss of her beloved son by stepping firmly into her Christian faith and determining to make a difference to other young people living in Manchester. I first met her at the Standing Together Against Violence event at Gorton Monastery, where we celebrated the miraculous recovery of another Sophie, Sophie Finucane–the West Gorton girl who recovered from a gunshot to the head. I've worked often since then with Patsy and others involved in Mothers Against Violence, the movement she set up to address the issues that were contributing to youth on youth violence on our streets.

Dorrie McKay & Sophie Lancaster

Sophie's mother, Sylvia, was already working in support of young people when her daughter's life was ended in an act of violence. Like Patsy, Sylvia channelled her powerful sense of loss towards helping other young people learn to show respect across expressions of identity. As Punk Monk, I met Sylvia when John Robb, Rob Haynes and I invited her to attend a Goldblade gig at Manchester Academy and tell the crowd about the Sophie Lancaster Foundation she had set up in Sophie's honour.

Her message is summed up in the S.O.P.H.I.E. wristbands that demonstrate the wearer's commitment to **S**tamp **O**ut **P**rejudice, **H**atred and **I**ntolerance **E**verywhere.

Punk Monk, Sylvia Lancaster and Kate Conboy address fans during a Stone Roses gig.

In subsequent years, many gathered to meet these courageous women and show them their support by taking part in Million Mothers Marches, which set off from All Saints before marching to Castlefield for an afternoon of free live entertainment with inspirational speakers and celebrity appearances.

Sylvia has gone to rejoin Sophie now, but her legacy is huge.

Author and Sylvia Lancaster, who founded the Sophie Lancaster Foundation in her daughter's memory.

Patsy McKay of Mothers Against Violence

Patsy and Sylvia ensured that much has been done to make Greater Manchester safer for young and old alike. As more people get behind the movement, we can work together to get closer to our goal of a city that is free from gang-related violence; a city in which respect crosses the generations and our children and grandchildren can play and learn together peacefully.

The Toy Store Line-up

Having assisted Katz when she was vulnerable, she'd sometimes run things by me when she came to work with vulnerable people herself. The day she rang about Riana, she'd tried everything she could think of.

"Dave, the teenager I'm with has been having a hard time and is at her wits' end. Right now her head is all over the place and all she wants to do is run away from it all. Can we come to see you?"

"I'm in town. Meet me at the toy store."

Waiting for Katz and Riana to arrive, I wandered around the aisles of the big toy store wondering how best to approach Riana's problem. If I gave her the "do you know how dangerous it is for young runaways?" spiel, I'd come across as just another adult with no idea what it was like being a kid in today's world. Perhaps I should meet her on familiar ground?

Spotting a sign advertising a new range of ethnic Barbie dolls, my light went on. By the time Katz and Riana arrived, I was on my knees in the aisle making a line of Barbie dolls. This was not what either expected, and, despite her troubles, Riana started to giggle at my crazy antics.

"What you doing?"

"Well, Katz", I responded, "I'm trying to see if this inclusive range of dolls has missed anyone out. There's Barbados Barbie, American Barbie, British Barbie, African Barbie, Asian Barbie and…" adding another doll to the lineup, "Chinese Barbie."

Katz knew I was up to something. Earlier, I'd spotted an officious-looking manager telling two children off for playing tag in the aisles. Any minute now he was going to spot me and unwittingly help young Riana sort her head out. It's great, once you've come to understand yourself, having an Asperger's mindset–but not always so good for by-the-book adults who cross your path. Right on cue, the suited manager came to stand over me.

"What's this then?" he growled, looking along the long line of dolls.

"A Barbie-Queue!" To his credit, hearing the obvious stated, he spluttered with laughter. The girls were in hysterics.

Moments later in the café upstairs, Riana was relaxed enough to tell her story to a complete stranger. I didn't need to advise her. Once her intelligent head was clear of turmoil, she stopped going around in circles and was capable of coming up with her own solutions. She used Katz and me to work out what to say to her family to begin the process of resolving certain pressures and rang to arrange to stay with an older sister until things had worked out.

Toys are designed to stimulate children's imaginations. Seeing a variety of model females change an unapproachable manager into a chuckling fluffy bunny was a piece of therapy Riana needed at that moment in her life. Play remains important in the adult world too.

The White Lady and the Lecturer

Back in the 1980s, our Lifeshare outreach teams came across several homeless guys who were sleeping near a warm air outlet over where the Printworks is now. There was one bloke, a small, wiry Scot we'll call 'Colin', who was usually well away when we arrived. He'd wake while we were chatting with the others and join us for a meal and a natter.

Colin had the smell of someone who'd been drinking 'White Lady' (meths) over a long period. Unlike the others, he'd never speak about how he acquired his demons.

One night, we negotiated with the lads for a TV documentary crew to come out with us later in the week to do some discreet filming to raise awareness around street homelessness. Colin hadn't woken up to join us, so had not been part of the discussion.

The night of filming arrived, and we were just setting up, when Colin woke startled. He looked like a rabbit in headlights under the lights that were being got ready before the cameras rolled.

"Oh, fuck!" He exclaimed, before staggering off into the night.

Two nights later, we found him again while parked in Piccadilly. For the first time, he was ready to get a place to live and sort out his demons.

"When I saw those cameras, I realised my mother might see me on TV and the shock could kill her", he said.

We used a telephone box to call an alcohol treatment unit, which agreed to offer Colin somewhere to begin his recovery. As he climbed into the back of the mini-bus, he started to tremble uncontrollably. He was clearly in distress. As the volunteer driver shut the doors, Colin screamed in sheer terror. He was fighting furiously, more with himself than with us. We held him and spoke with him reassuringly. I'd seen a lot of things, but I don't think I'd seen fear like that before that night, though sadly I've seen it many times since.

We visited Colin in the alcohol treatment unit. He was doing amazingly well. Then he simply fell off our radar and we didn't see him again for ages.

When the invite came to attend a talk on alcohol, recovery, myself and a couple of volunteers were eager to attend. Though I'd worked on ATUs while training in mental health a decade earlier, there were always new things to learn. Little did any of us realise what we were going to learn in this lecture.

When we arrived, we were told seats had been reserved for us up front.

The place was packed and some of the most eminent folk in the medical, psychiatric and rehab professions were in attendance. There was a panel of speakers on the stage sitting behind microphones, while a smartly dressed gentleman who seemed to be in charge was settling everyone in and making sure their microphones were working.

At last, he stepped forward.

"Some of you know me as a motivational speaker, but that has not always been my role in life. In fact…" and suddenly his voice changed, and the light began to dawn on us… "It's thanks to that motley crew down there", he pointed to us, "that I'm here at all. If they hadn't disturbed my alcoholic slumber one night by inviting a TV documentary crew down to where I was sleeping rough, I might be dead now…"

It was Colin. We slid down our seats sheepishly.

"Sit up!" he said, to ripples of laughter. "I'm not accusing you–I want to thank you. The thought of my mother seeing the state her son had gotten into galvanised me to change the course of my life and I sought help. You were the first to help me, but there have been others since."

He went on to describe how he had been in and out of prison and gotten in with the wrong people. One night in a city far away, he had gotten into a van with members of a gang he'd been involved in. As he did so, he realised that another of the gang members was trussed up terrified. That night, the people he'd been hanging about with shot the other man dead in the back of the van right in front of him. When he could, he had fled as far away as possible and tried to numb his mind with drink, until in the end he was sleeping rough and taking comfort with the 'white lady'.

He spoke of how that first step we had encouraged him to take into an ATU had been the start of a long and difficult journey.

At the end of the evening, Colin came to see us. The changes we saw in him were incredible to see. Post-Traumatic Stress Disorder (PTSD) can arise in many situations and can lead to all sorts of complications. It takes great courage to fight back to regain your life again, but it can take a lot of non-judgemental encouragement, occasionally a chance set of circumstances, before a person realises they have what it takes to make the journey.

Collywobbles

'Collette' was sixteen when she applied to become a Lifeshare volunteer. Our policy was eighteen plus, and only then after we'd sifted out the rescuers and supported people through a preparation process to ensure they would not be overwhelmed. Even then, we would have an extra hand volunteer experienced enough to peel off with a first-time outreach worker who found their initial encounter with the realities of abject poverty, exploitation or abuse so shocking they needed time to adjust.

Colly, as Colette preferred to be called, showed such promise that we offered to train her to be part of the less demanding daytime outreach when we would meet homeless folk for a chat in a café or move among the scores of pensioners who spent their days sitting in the Arndale in Thatcherite Britain, because a bus into town was far less costly than heating their own homes.

One day, we were in Chorlton Street Bus Station café having a brew before we finished our shift, when some of the women from our red-light tea-break team came in. We put tables together so we could chat and share news.

As it dawned on Colly that these women offered a 'tea-break' to women who, in those days when none knew better, were at best referred to as sex workers; gave them condoms and advice on staying safe, alongside options for getting out if they were ready to move on, she expressed surprise.

When Colly made a comment that was out of character, I realised her instincts for helping others were rooted in personal trauma.

Because of her age, Colly had been assigned two mentors, whom the volunteers referred to as 'Cagney' and 'Lacey'. As I and her mentors drove her home that day to the unusually spacious and cosy garret above her grandparents' house, Colly poured out her story. She spoke lovingly of her mother and the brother from whom she had become estranged, and then she told us about a male relative in the extended family circle who had sexually abused her.

"I've been through hell, but I'd never dream of selling myself for sex!" she said vehemently.

We knew that now the scab had been removed from her wound, Colly was going to need a lot of support.

Over the next few months, Cagney and Lacey met regularly with Colly to help her through her issues. Then, one night, I got a frantic phone call. It was Colly's mother who, with Cagney and Lacey's guidance, Colly had been reunited. She couldn't get hold of Cagney or Lacey and she knew no one else she could turn to. Colly was in a very dark place and her mother feared for the life of the daughter she had only recently been reconciled with. I heard Colly scream in the background.

"I'm on my way."

When Colly's younger brother opened the door, I surveyed a scene of carnage. The walls were smeared with blood and a large kitchen knife had, judging by the blood trails, been kicked spinning into a corner. Her mother was holding Colly in her arms in the middle of the floor, but when mum looked up to greet me, Colly used the distraction to make a frantic leap for the window with a clear intention to throw herself through the glass to the street below.

Pushing past her brother, I leapt across the room to grab her and pin her to the floor, using my weight to stop her from completing her intention. Colly was kicking and screaming under me, while her mother and brother stood nearby shocked into immobility.

As Colly squirmed beneath my weight I started crying. Slowly, I realised she had stopped struggling. I couldn't look at her but was terrified of letting her go. Then her voice, now calm and somewhat curious, broke my reverie.

"Why are you crying?"

"Because I truly care about you and respect you, but I know that as a man pinning you down like this, I remind you of every time you were violated. I never, ever wanted to remind you of that. But if I get up and you leap through that window, the bastards win."

I felt her relax under me, then realised she too was crying.

"Look at me", she pleaded.

Gazing down at her, I now saw a tranquil Colly looking back at me with something akin to pity, mingled with regret that she'd put me in this situation. Of course, she hadn't. That responsibility lay with someone else altogether whom I had never met.

Slowly, as we empathetically read each other, her mother came across to hold her daughter. Out of the corner of my eye, I saw her brother sink into a chair, relieved that his cherished sister was going to be okay.

When Colly agreed to go to the hospital, we travelled there in my car.

When we were met at reception by a judgemental woman who had neither the empathy nor the experience to see Colly as anything other than a self-harmer, Colly stepped over a threshold.

"Thank you", she told the unhelpful receptionist. "As a woman who can't see the suffering of other women, you have helped me realise that it's not only men who help the harm to continue in society. You will never see me again, but I will be out there being what you can never be for other women."

Later back at the garret, her brother cleaned up while mum and I cauterised the lacerations on Colly's arms and bandaged them with purchases from an all-night chemist.

Wincing at the stinging antiseptic, Colly turned to me.

"Thank you. I'm glad Cagney and Lacey weren't around tonight. I've always loved my brother here, but I've never trusted another man for a long time." She smiled and I knew she was going to be okay.

When Colly went to Bristol to volunteer with an excellent women's project, she stayed in touch with her three Lifeshare friends. A few years later, I bumped into her during a seminar at which she was speaking. To the surprise of the women with her, she lit up and gave me a hug, before introducing me as her “only male friend”, describing me as “almost a woman”. As if she’d spoken a codeword, they relaxed and joined in the chat.

Colly kept her promise to that unhelpful casualty receptionist. She is still out there empowering other women and girls and helping law enforcement agencies take abusive men who traffic women and children out of circulation.

PART 4

CELLS: MONASTERIES, PRISONS AND FAMOUS PRISONERS

During our efforts to restore Gorton Monastery, we did a lot of work around restorative justice. Inspired by the friars' community orchard, on our smallholding, we grew fruit and vegetables to supply outreach projects and drop-in centres and rescued hens, ducks and geese to get up to 6,000 eggs into the diets of pensioners and other vulnerable people. My wife, Elaine, managed this project, which depended on volunteers and people doing community service on probation.

I and other team members also worked with prisoners, whether in several Northwest prisons or through day-release agreements with HMP Buckley Hall, which was then a female prison.

One day while giving a talk about the early days of the monastery, a prison governor in attendance who remembered me from the Strangeways riots informed me that HMP Strangeways and Gorton Monastery were built around the same time from bricks made of clay quarried in the same area, the place my grandfather had once worked.

This selection of standalone stories comes from these times. The first is a reminder of the problems that repeat throughout history when a society takes its eyes off the needs of children and young people or comes to see them merely as economic units or even cannon fodder.

The Mancy Scuttlers–an Insight from Second World War Veterans

When The Smiths created one of Sally-Manc-Music's best-loved icons, they did so in the energy of a much older egregore, that of the 'Mancy Scuttler's'–turf gangs whose violence inspired fear and loathing across the industrial landscape of nineteenth-century Manchester.

The Scuttlers were a symptom of a culture that had failed to meet the play, leisure and gainful engagement needs of children and young people. A harsh judicial approach didn't change the zeitgeist, though the provision of lads' clubs like the Adelphi did make a difference. The transformation of the Scuttlers into friendly competitors ended the violent youth culture. Despite this lesson of history, young people were again let down across post-slum-clearance Manchester and inevitably a new era of youth-on-youth violence erupted. Insightful approaches have regained some ground, but our journey back to wholeness is not yet complete.

Hearteningly, the fastest-growing youth gang in Manchester today stands for equality across diversity. With 1,000+ Goth, Punk, Atheist, Jewish, Indie, Muslim, Buddhist, Christian, Straight, Gay and so forth members, "Queerstianity" has a wholesome message of cooperation.

While individuals stand in their own power, young people collectively assert the rights of all to autonomy and identity.

As we re-embrace the wisdom of nurture, let's hope that the young people leading us all into a new paradigm of mutual regard are spared the fate of their Scuttler predecessors, which I've tried to outline in the verse below.

The Mancy Scuttlers

We've grown up in the city Where there's little joy of green
and the lark and mellow Mistle Thrush are neither heard nor seen.
We eke out our existence in a cloud of poison smog
and the rhythm of our heartbeats is the shuffling of clogs.
O, we are the Mancy Scuttler's who you wouldn't want to meet
for we'd fight you on the brick crofts and we'd fight you in the streets.
We slash, thump, belt and bludgeon, our anger to dispel
and if you are not one of us, we'll give you bloody hell!

A great need of belonging sits in every human heart
alongside pride in family and the neighbours of your hearth.
We do not feel so lonely or believe that life's all grim
when, belts off, we are scuttling with enemies and friends.

When came the Salford Lads Club and the club at Ardwick too;

the ones across in Cheetham and in Collyhurst and Hulme
we regained a sense of purpose that enabled us to say:
"Though I used to scuttle with you, shall we have a snooker game?"

O, we were the Mancy Scuttlers who now box and football play
now society looks out for us and helps us change our ways.
We're all pals together and we'll go scuttling no more -
we're too busy forming regiments, for the world has gone to war.

Royal Air Force Peace Mala

Teacher Pam Evans developed the Peace Mala bracelet after 9/11 to promote respect across spectrums of faith and culture in schools. The idea spread. Now the Dali Lama, Archbishop of York and Terry Waite have joined school children and thousands of adults from all walks of life in wearing the multi-coloured beads to show their commitment to the whole human family. I've worn one for a number of years, along with Poppy and S.O.P.H.I.E. wristbands.

The author (left), Elaine Griffiths MBE, ex-Guardsman and negotiator, Terry Waite CBE at the RAF Peace Mala event at the monastery that David and Elaine helped see restored.

Working around realigning Manchester gang culture, I've had the profound honour of meeting scores of young people who accepted support from caring adults to develop alternatives to the self and soul-destroying patterns that were once destroying young lives in our city. One group of young men joined an intensive team-building programme that offered alternative models for gang structuring that were marked by respect and cooperation rather than division and rivalry. On the first day, when they were still growlingly suspicious of each other and our adult intention, they asked those of us with Peace Mala's why we were wearing "girly bracelets".

After organising a music gig together and other team-building stuff over several weeks, we dropped into a Royal Air Force (RAF) base in Lincolnshire to see how much they had grown. The RAF really put them through their paces with climbing, abseiling and other team-building activities. But the thing I'll never forget is the way they learned to handle dangerous equipment.

"This here is a phosphorous flare", the Flight Sergeant was saying.

"I'm wearing this thick glove because if it slips in my hand, it will burn through my skin and bone instantly."

After igniting his flare at arm's length, he turned to the lads. "Right, they come in various colours and when you stand in line and let yours off, there will be no protective gloves, so be VERY careful. You have to be responsible when handling dangerous situations."

When the boys formed a chatty huddle around the flight sergeant, we adults wondered if they were intimidated by the potential danger. When the RAF man disappeared inside an ammo shed with the box of flares, we were sure the exercise had been called off. We needn't have worried. The flight sergeant reappeared with another box of flares, and soon the lads stood in line at the ready. One of the lads turned our way: "This is for you, Rainbow Warriors", he called.

As they took an arm's length, eyes averted, position, and let their flares off across an open field, our hearts filled with pride to see how far they'd come, which was evident in how they'd asked the flight sergeant to change the white flares for different coloured flares and worked together to ensure they were in position to produce a spectacular Peace Mala rainbow across the field.

A team parachute jump couldn't top this!

Only frightened young people carry knives and guns. We knew these boys would never be afraid again. Since then, I've developed a closer working relationship with the RAF and am delighted to have been invited to become a chaplain in relation to their excellent work with young people.

The Miracle of Sophie Finucane and Struggle for Young Lives

Just above Sister Pauline's socks box in the laundry room of Mary and Joseph House hung a picture of Padre Pio. While distributing fresh clothing to homeless men with an amazing wounded healer named Ann who is hidden away elsewhere in this book, I would often wonder about the miracles claimed for this saint. Little did I realise then that one day, from beyond death, he and I would share roles in another miracle.

A few years ago, I read a report in the *Manchester Evening News* about a West Gorton teenager who had been shot in the head at close range. She was, the report said, on life-support under police protection. Her name was not given. As the police normally told me about incidents likely to cause distress to my community, I was surprised they hadn't called me. Four days later, a small snippet named the victim: Sophie Finucane. My eyes filled with tears. I'd known Sophie since she was six years old. Because West Gorton is in the Ardwick ward, someone in Greater Manchester Police (GMP) had failed to realise she lived in my community. When I rang GMP to request that the family liaison officer check if I could visit, there was a troubled pause. When my phone rang a few minutes later, I understood why: the person ringing was not a family liaison officer but a family bereavement officer. Sophie was considered dead. The life-support was a loving courtesy to her family as they came to terms with their pain.

Within the hour, I was standing beside Sophie's bed. Her father John had pleaded with me, "Ask God for my girl back now!" His faith was to prove a conduit for divine healing that would amaze and inspire thousands. With medical staff standing in support as Dad and I each held one of Sophie's hands, I spoke to the universe:

"Father-Mother God, too many children are dying needlessly in this city. They are your children too. You know what it's like to watch your son suffer. But you gave us free will and would not send one of your beloved back from the safety of Paradise against their will to a world that had treated them so cruelly. Please give this father the courage to face whatever must be–but if his girl wants to come back, will you let her?"

At that moment, Sophie squeezed her father's hand. A few days later she was sitting up and talking with her family. The miracle of Sophie Finucane played a significant part in changing gang culture in this city–and despite subsequent setbacks, many hope we are moving towards lasting change.

There's little space to tell it all here, but it's a story that needs to be heard in these times of despair. It is a wonderful story of a father's faith, a child's humility, a saint's touch and a community's healing.

The day before John had rung me to tell me Sophie would live, I'd penned the following in response to an outpouring of grief from young people on social media. Seems someone listened.

A Rap on Heaven's Door:

Father–Mother God, you know it's true:
That things go wrong when we turn from you.
I've known this child since she was six,
but you've known her since the very first bricks
of the universe were called in place,
you know her name and you know her face;
You know each cell in her heart and soul
and you know she's strong and more precious than gold.
No child of yours deserves this fate,
bring us all to our senses before it's too late.
Forgive we elders who have let the young bloods down
by failing to show them the common ground
where life is precious and all are of worth
who breathe your air and walk your earth.
Pour out your grace on the human race
so we can all pull together and build a better place,
where children play and learn and grow,
hate, drug, guns and knives all unknown;
Where all can stand in their own esteem
to reclaim again the Eden dream
of a garden filled with food for all
where each one again can hear you call
their name in deep, amazing love

as they walk among the fruitful groves
that you prepared for all of us
where the streams of loving mercy flow.
Look kindly on Sophie's father John
and ease the heart of her mum, Sharon;
comfort her friends and family;
Bless Cedar Mount School with harmony.
You are working through those who have her care
in a city where folk are so aware
that our Children need a guiding hand
to end the violence and truly honour the gangs.
From the Street Pastors to every church and mosque;
Charisma to each synagogue;
from temple, shrine to Gujarat
in our streets and homes is where you' at.
Unite us so we don't reject
the gifts of life and of respect.
If it is your will that Sophie come
to the safety of your own kingdom
then help us all to realise
that the way of peace is the way to life.
Mothers Against Violence
Fathers Against Strife
Children for Freedom, for Justice
and Life.
Yet, you can Heal this girl in every way,
with such a powerful message so that all may say:
"We've trod the wrong path long enough,
let's get back on the Way of Love".
Be with her, Lord. Thy will be done
for Sophie and for everyone
who sends out love and healing prayer
revealing that your world still cares.
Thank you for what you can achieve
through a single life that is bold and free;
Thank you for the life she's known
but thank you more for what is yet to come.

In the hospital, John had made a divine promise to help me in my efforts to address the gang culture that had almost claimed his daughter's life. When Sophie's father kept that promise, something was set in motion that saved many lives and took gang violence in Manchester down by an incredible 97%.

It began when we held an event at Gorton Monastery.

I was secretary to Faith Network for Manchester at the time and was delighted when leaders from Judaism, Islam, Hinduism, Jainism, Bahai, Christianity, Paganism, Buddhism, Humanism, Atheism, Sikhism and Taoism showed a packed gathering of young people, police officers, teachers, parents and others that people with very different backgrounds could achieve more working together than playing silly games like postcode territorialism or "my god's bigger than your god".

We touched on the deep grief of our communities, in which many young people had been killed in gang violence. We began with a song of gratitude, *Day's* sung by The Kinks, during which bunches of flowers were handed to mothers whose children had been killed. Before a large poster of the iconic *Manchester Evening News* front page collage made up of the faces of young people killed needlessly, we prayed for them and our city. Then, in the restored sacred space of Gorton Monastery the resurrected person of Sophie Finucane was introduced to the people.

When John spoke of how he was incredibly lucky to still have his daughter, the atmosphere was powerfully energised.

Afterwards, a group of young people came to speak with me. They said they had been enemies until now but wanted to work together to change outcomes for themselves and other young people. Tenor Martin Toal, who could claim that when he sang to open England matches, the England team always won, was passing. I grabbed his arm. "Martin, will you help?" He agreed. Kadria Thomas, who had worked with Stevie Wonder and taken choirs into prison with me also got on board, as did a dance choreographer and a youth worker whom some of the young people knew and trusted.

One of the lads had busked in Manchester and was expressing in rap what his generation was going through. United the skills of the young people and the concerned adults, we wrote and organised a show, *Streetwise*, that opened at Sophie's old school. In the audience was a recently released young man who had been to prison after finding a gun his mother had been forced to hide and accidentally shot and killed his sister. His despair found something to surf as he watched other young people perform, dance and sing about the troubles he had thought he was alone with.

Other initiatives followed:

- Faith Network 4 Manchester (FN4M) organised a dinner entitled: 'My Gang = My Family', to which we invited gang members, decision-makers, law enforcement professionals and others to eat together and share ideas going forward.
- A gun amnesty took hundreds of firearms out of circulation, including a gun handed in at one of my church services.
- Mothers Against Violence organised the Million Mothers March.
- Street Pastors, United Estates of Wythenshawe and Carisma were just some of the organisations working together to make a difference, inspiring other UK cities and communities around the world.
- President Barack Obama sent his people to meet with us at Manchester Town Hall in his efforts to gain insights as to how to deal with gun violence in the United States.

When my then fourteen-year-old grandson, Liam, and his mates formed the biggest gang of them all–Queerstianity–it was one of the proudest moments of my life.

Liam Callacher, author's grandson, with founding members of Queerstianity and Goldblade 2007.

In an effort to counter the hate messages of street evangelists, who were at the time targeting Muslim and gay young people on their way through the city from school, Queerstianity gathered children and young people who were being bullied because of their skin colour, size, ability, faith, culture, sexuality and a range of other ridiculous excuses to make young lives a misery. Soon a thousand strong, the movement organised peaceful protests, got the hate preachers moved on by the police and began forming bands to raise funds for Amnesty International and other causes.

My FN4M friends, Jonny Wineberg, and Muslim writer, Qaisra Shahraz, put them in for a Diana Award, which we presented them with in the centre of the city they had helped to heal. When Liam went on to win a Homo Hero Award, part of his prize was to lead that year's Pride Parade with Sir Ian McKellen, because of his age he had to be accompanied by an adult. "Who will you ask?"

"Well, if I'm to walk with Gandalf the Grey, there's only one person I can ask. My Grandad the Gray", was his reply.

That turned out an amazing Pride parade. When we got to the part of the route where the hate preachers were spewing their toxic hate, Liam, Gandalf and I addressed the crowd around them:

"Mancunians! Like Hobbits, you bow to no one!"

FN4M went on to organise 'Faithful Storytelling" and "In Your Faith" sessions in schools and youth organisations. In my Franciscan habit, I'd be accompanied by Jewish, Sikh, and Muslim friends, among others, to tell stories from the faiths to primary school children or hold debates with high school and youth group members, including Air, Sea and Army Cadets.

Feedback from evaluation forms completed by participants showed an overall positive experience. While we were not there to proselytise or compete, but to promote a better understanding of the faiths and, while highlighting differences, to demonstrate common factors such as the Golden Rule, some young people expressed an interest in deepening their own faith practice. While one student, for example, asked to be put in touch with his local church to explore baptism, another wished to know where he could learn more about Islam. In one of the youth groups, two young people said they had enjoyed the presentations on the Abrahamic Faiths and would now like to know more about Hinduism as they had Hindu friends and wanted to know more about their faith practice. In consultation with their adult leaders, a decision was reached to invite the Hindu friends to come and address the group personally, with support from FN4M.

Delighted to be invited to speak at the Diversity Gold Awards ceremony at Manchester Town Hall one year, I was even more pleased to learn that no less than sixteen Manchester Schools had earned this prestigious national accolade, among them schools that had invited FN4M to work with them in nurturing cooperation and respect while inspiring citizenship and community cohesion.

Our 'In Your Faith' team was so successful in High Schools, FN4M decided to build on previous work with primary schools, including poultry and allotment workshops through our Growing Faith in Community smallholding.

There were many other initiatives aimed at reducing youth tension, but one that will always shine out for me is the Sophie Lancaster Foundation.

Sophie had been murdered in a park in Bacup by a gang of youths who took exception to her alternative lifestyle culture. Sophie was a Goth. Her mother, Sylvia, and her friend, Kate, worked tirelessly to spread a message of respect and understanding in Sophie's honour, with the slogan S.O.P.H.I.E. (**S**tamp **O**ut **P**rejudice **H**atred and **I**ntolerance **E**verywhere).

As Punk Monk, the Bez-like novelty item (only teasing Bez) with John Robb's punk band Goldblade, I was privileged to work closely with Sylvia and Kate at concerts involving bands like The Damned, Stone Roses and The Membranes.

When Sylvia died in 2022 and we laid her to rest with Sophie, the wonderful human beings who followed her coffin up the cemetery hill included the great and the good from film, music, and the arts, alongside police officers, politicians and a full range of humanity. Our friend, the astonishingly gifted actress, Julie Hesmondhalgh, who had played Sylvia in dramatisations of Sophie's story, was also present. Gold Blade's drummer Rob Hayes, Kate and I wondered why, with all that energy going towards the side of the angels, the society Sylvia had struggled so hard to achieve was still so elusive. It's sad what a change of government can do to police-community relations. We parted agreeing to keep our eye on the ball.

Old Dogs and Raptors

One night in West Gorton a few years back, our old dog, Bruce, woke and led me downstairs. Activating the garden light, he revealed a hungry Vixen foraging on our lawn. When she led me to her cubs, we were able to help her feed them. Bruce's concern for a wild sister inspired me to further open my heart to the wilder members of my human community, who are often disregarded.

Now I've always enjoyed the company of raptors: the eagles that soared above our officer's quarters during past regimental camps; the kites accompanying Stephanie and me on a recent spiritual journey; the golden eagle that brushed my hair during my ascent of a Scottish Ben.

Bob the Buzzard and his wife, Pat, who did the Belle Vue Zoological Gardens' animal feeds, had a legendary affinity with Raptors. Bob, an inventive surgeon, once made a new beak from a plastic pen top for a bird that had lost its own. Though it could feed itself, it remained in captivity, as the prosthetic beaks needed replacing regularly.

The book about the couple, who lived in Gorton until the time came for me to do their funerals (I still have the ceremonial sword used for both services, for Bob and Pat were Pagans) is called *Kestrels in the Kitchen*. It's a great read.

Another Bob, Robert Stroud–'The Birdman of Alcatraz', opened judicial minds to new possibilities in prisoner management. With a small number of lifers who cannot be released in the public interest, Raptor companions are sometimes offered. Something profoundly spiritual is communicated in the sense of freedom the flight of the bird affords those entrusted with their care.

During a prison visit a few years ago with one of Gorton Monastery's artists, we spent the day teaching angel moulding skills to three prisoners from North and East Manchester. Among the items Anne had brought for the session was a stone-mould oyster-catcher.

The prisoners were fascinated by the technique that turned its dull stone into a bronze finish with glimmering wings. They were most enthusiastic as they applied the technique on stone-cast angels, opening up to talk about those things that had made them prisoners of habit before ever going into custody.

By handling things of beauty made more beautiful by their own hands, these lads were learning to realise the power of using their skills constructively. When three governors joined us as observers, they too were inspired and remained to share a sandwich lunch with us. When the governors asked if they could visit the Monastery, they didn't bat an eye when I suggested that the lads might like to make the journey with them to get a better feel as to how what they did in the prison workshop impacted positively on their home community.

As well as running a prison art competition in the run-up to restoration, prisoners played a bigger part in the revival of Gorton Monastery than many people realise. Those who offend in a community are often the symptoms of its problems. Creating space to change their outlook is an essential aspect where seeking solutions is concerned.

The Jesus Insight

It would seem odd to have a book about wounded healers that didn't mention the most famous wounded healer of all, especially as he is a Jungian archetype for all wounded healers. As there is much that points to his also being an Aspie, how can I not mention Jesus.

For me, Jesus is far more powerful when we are able to avoid deifying him. Indeed, we can better see his divinity when we look first to his humanity.

As a community activist, Jesus, having wrestled with his own psyche in the wilderness after meeting his spirit animal, the dove, after undergoing the rebirthing immersion ritual with John; goes on to be the shaman who guides his followers towards their own spiritual growth. He tells them: "The kingdom of heaven is within you", so pointing them towards their own humanity and divinity. He stresses with Aspie clarity that our family are those who see us as who we are and accept us for who we are, going on to reveal all the flaws of the religious-political system of his age and showing that attitudes such as racism, exclusion, misogyny, prejudice and a sense of self-righteousness bordering on entitlement point away rather than towards wholesome society, or the kingdom of G*d as he called it.

When he is confronted by military, religious and political power, he doesn't recognise its authority (very Aspie), but in clever ways holds a mirror to it that in many cases leads to those seeking to win an argument with him to back off.

When he is asked: are you the son of G*d?" His reply is very revealing to those who have eyes and ears, "You say that I am."

Imagine his exasperation. He has pointed out that we are all of us, from the powerful to the weak; lepers and other outsiders; women and children, sons and daughters of G*d, but still when he stands in his own humanity and divinity, those before him can't take the next logical step. Having discovered his "I Am", he can never again let it go. But still, he points others to "We Are", showing them the road to satori but leaving it to them to decide whether they will sweat it.

What a wonderful insight he offers Jairus, a leader of the synagogue, when Jairus begged him to come and heal his daughter. On the way to Jairus house to see the child, he draws attention to the woman who has touched the hem of his garment. He asks her to tell him and the crowd what has happened. She explains that she is now healed of a bleeding illness that had long prevented her from entering the temple sacred space due to strict Levitical laws. We are not told whether Jairus understood that in healing this daughter of the faith, Jesus was pointing to how the whole community might be healed. By the time Jesus arrives at Jairus house, he is told the little girl has died. Neither her story nor the story ends there.

This is not the place to go into detail regarding something that is caught up in the maelstrom of religion. Though I'm a priest, I don't do religion anymore, it gets in the way of deeper meaning. Still, we must say something of this man who knew and accepted who he was and would never deny that understanding regardless of the threats the world made against his physical self. He was willing to embrace a painful death rather than become the lesser self that powerful forces were demanding him to be.

The power of Jesus as an iconic wounded healer is that he goes on to show his wounds to his friends.

"Look! I've recovered from these wounds, so why do you fear? You too can recover from whatever wounds life inflicts on you."

Later, one of his friends is able to say:

"I Am persuaded that neither death, nor life, nor angels, nor principalities, nor powers, nor things present, nor things to come; nor height, nor depth, nor any other creature, shall be able to separate us from the love of G*d."

Putting such confidence into practice can be very challenging for those who, having been wounded, are healing themselves and others.

In my own experience, each time you stand in the fullness of your integrity, though it may seem that all security and even life itself may be falling away, you emerge from the storm as if on eagle wings to take another step up above the turmoil.

St. Francis asked and in due course received. He is thought to be the first stigmata, a person whose body is wounded in the places Jesus was wounded when nailed to a cross with a crown of thorns on his head and a spear thrust into his side. Interestingly for me, Francis also shows signs of having been what, today, we call an Aspie. He seems to have totally got the Jesus insight, coming to understand inclusive love way beyond his famous encounter with a leper. At a time of the Crusade, he spoke to pope and sultan about this inclusive love, reminding them of the story of Ishmael and G*ds acceptance of someone the Abrahamic family of faith patriarchs and matriarchs rejected, possibly removing the sting of justification from the insanity of crusaders and jihadists alike. He went further. In an age when Pagans were feared and persecuted by the church, Francis communed with animals and wrote magnificent Pagan prayers, such as his famous Canticle to Brother Sun.

PART 5

PADRE TALES

Dunkirk Spirit

The late and legendary Mike Williams roped me into becoming a padre. Before ageing membership obliged them to hang up their colours, Emmanuel Gorton, where Mike was Rector, was the Dunkirk Veterans' Association's regimental chapel. During one of their annual services, Mike was sharing his wealth of knowledge in a lengthy sermon when the veteran next to me leaned over and whispered, "I wish the small boats would come and rescue me from this ruddy sermon!"

When I told Mike, he simply said: "You do it next year!"

Stepping up to preach the following year, I removed my shoes and asked: "Is the gentleman who prayed the small boats would rescue him from last year's sermon here?"

"I'm here, lad!"

"Then fear not! Like Moses, I've removed my footwear, for before you I stand on holy ground. I've spent my life seeking faith to know that no matter how tough things get, the divine offers a way out. No one represents that depth of faith in modern times more than you, for the God who parted the Red Sea to save the Israelites from the Egyptian Army, is the same God who sent the small boats to get the British Expeditionary Force back across the Channel from Dunkirk. This snot-nosed kid will sit down now, before your sandwiches start to curl and your pints go flat in the barrack's mess. There's nothing I can teach you–for you are the sermon today. I salute you!"

I sat down in deathly silence, Mike peering at me curiously. Suddenly there was a cheering round of applause.

At the end of the service, a rotund Polish general and his batman approached me.

"You will be our chaplain!"

"As I'm not due to be ordained for at least a year, the bishop won't allow it", was my response.

I never found out what the general said, but within the week I had a letter from Bishopscourt confirming me as chaplain to Federation des Combatants Allies en Europe, attached to the Polish Reserve Independent Brigade.

Thus, my adventures as a veterans' chaplain began. As well as supporting local regiments old boys' networks, I was also invited to, in little ways, serve Royal Air Force and Royal Navy veterans, and the forces cadet networks. Then, invited as padre on battlefield pilgrimages alongside First and Second World War veterans. I began meeting members of the Dutch, French, Norwegian, Polish and other resistance movements that had fought fascism in the 20th Century.

D-Day veteran, Rowley, with wife, Flo, and Federation of Allied Combatants secretary, Mo Shields, and her son, Pete, during one of the author's battlefield pilgrimages.

These days, with all the First World War veterans gone to the re-muster, and with so few Second World War veterans still alive, my role as padre is restricted to local regiments like the Manchester Regiment, Stockport and Manchester Royal Artillery Association and of course the Cheshire Regiment, who, as a biker, have welcomed me into their 22nd Riders group.

It was while sharing a table at a regimental dinner that I had the pleasure to have a curious conversation with Stan Gore, since gone to his reward, who served with the Royal Artillery and was a Dunkirk veteran.

Stan, having recalled my sermon to the Dunkirk Veterans'

Association, told me how he'd celebrated his 21st birthday with his artillery battery holding a rear-guard action at Dunkirk. Thinking he wouldn't live to see another birthday; he'd overheard a despatch read to his commanding officer.

"Fear not! The whole of the British nation is at prayer. God will look after you." It was from the King himself.

"When I heard those words", Stan said, "I knew I'd see England again. Operation Dynamo was mobilised. The rest is history."

My grandfather told me a similar tale of how the nation had prayed during a dark hour of the First World War. The next day, superior German forces had surrendered to surprised Tommys.

"We thought we'd defeat you", the German prisoners of war confided, "until came your White Cavalry looking like invincible Angels!"

"Have you ever read 2 Kings Chapter 6?", my grandfather had asked. "We had no White Cavalry."

Going Dutch

A number of Manchester lads took part in Operation Market Garden during the Second World War. Much of their parachute training for the drop into occupied Holland took place at Manchester Airport (RAF Ringway). My Uncle Cyril grew up in Cheetham Hill and worked at Connelly's Cables in Crumpsall. When war broke out, he became an RAF Navigator. Cyril's plane was shot down during Market Garden– the Battle for Holland. The crew were killed. Only one soldier travelling in the glider they had been towing survived.

Mum and Gran told me Cyril's story when I was a small boy. They spoke of his growing up with a great love of animals, which he shared with my beloved Uncle Walter who, because of deafness following a boyhood accident, served in the Home Guard. They shared how that surviving soldier came to see them and how, during a visit to Cyril's grave after the war, they met a leader of the Dutch Resistance.

Growing up, I was often shown a photograph of the Dutch Resistance leader and told how his teenage daughter had helped the surviving soldier hide in the swimming pool of the Hartenstein Hotel, which had been the German Headquarters until the Allied paratroopers started to fall from the sky when, the Germans having fled, it became Allied Headquarters all too briefly. Today, it is the Airborne Museum that tells the story of the brave men and women who resisted fascism during Market Garden. It had reverted to Nazi control after the operation failed, as outlined in Cornelius Ryan's famous book, *A Bridge Too Far*, which is an excellent account of the Battle for Holland.

My first visit to Cyril's grave was in 1972, with Uncle Walter and young Olwyn, who was in the process of becoming my sister.

Years earlier when we still lived in Marsland Street, so I was not yet seven, I had dreamed that I was standing by Cyril's grave with Walter and a child, who had a bag from which a cloth doll protruded. As we were at the grave, Olwyn suddenly put her bag down, and a rag doll she had purchased earlier that day lopped out of the side.

During battlefield pilgrimages with veterans, it was my humbling honour to not only visit Arnhem on a number of occasions and, as well as paying my respects to Cyril, lead acts of remembrance at Oosterbeek War Cemetery, where he now rests.

For one such occasion, I'd accompanied Polish veteran, Peter Blenco, when we went to buy wreaths before leaving Manchester to go on the battlefield pilgrimage to Arnhem. At Oosterbeek, having laid our wreaths, we stood up and stepped back to salute. Turning, we realised that our respective uncles were immediately across from one another. No wonder we had been becoming such close friends. But this was not the end of the cosmic serendipity at play that day.

Later, as we were enjoying beers and a lunch of frikandellen and fries at a restaurant near the Airborne Museum, a Dutch lady sitting at a table nearby asked one of the SAS lads who the padre was. When he mentioned that my uncle was buried at Oosterbeek, she came over to ask my uncle's name, registering surprise when I told her. Reaching into her handbag, she had produced a photograph.

"Do you know this man?"

Looking back at me was the face of the Dutch Resistance leader of all those years ago.

"Yes, my grandmother always cherished his photograph."

As was revealed on an episode of the TV cookery show *Flavours from Abroad*, in which Peter Blenco and I spoke of that day while TV cook Lesley Waters cooked us a meal of frikandellen and fries, it was truly magical and quite astonishing to meet this heroine of tales I'd heard at mum and Gran's knees as a small boy. In the woman I gazed at that day above an image of her father, I was talking to the young girl who had hidden an allied soldier in a swimming pool. As our eyes mingled, I could see our memories mingle and a mutual emotion pass between us. We both glistened with tears of recognition that no one else saw.

Danny Hoy was with us that day too. He'd been about seventeen when he and his pals got cut off from their regiment and had to be helped back down the lines by the Dutch Resistance.

A few years later at Oosterbeek one September, Danny was present when someone asked a Dutch groundsman what lay behind a high wall we had passed on our way into the cemetery. The friendly man showed us a gate and led us into the Dutch civilian cemetery. Spotting Danny looking at a row of graves, I was walking towards him when he took off up the road to be alone. When I got to the graves he had been looking at, I found in line the last resting places of ordinary Dutch people, including a local doctor, an old woman in her eighties and a baby held in his mother's arms, who had been shot by the Nazis because the Dutch people had helped our soldiers escape.

I hurried after Danny.

"I didn't know, padre", he said when I caught up with him. "The Dutch people have always welcomed us back and never mentioned what they suffered for helping us."

His old face streamed with the tears of painful memory.

The following year, British regimental networks placed a monument outside the Hartenstein Airborne Museum expressing the gratitude of British warriors to the Dutch people, who had risked so much to help liberate Europe in its greatest hour of need. Danny has since gone to his reward in eternity. I will never forget the kind, gentle man I knew or the courageous boy that had forged him.

Ukrainian Opera Detour

Some years ago, a Manchester Regiment delegation to France invited me along as padre. Due at Manchester Hill the next day, we spent our last evening in the bar, getting into a singing contest with four Ukrainian opera singers staying in the same billet. Jimmy, sadly now gone from our fellowship, had no tongue but earned a standing ovation for his guttural version of *Lili Marlene.* Wandering around the gathering, my eyes came to rest on a Dunkirk veteran sitting in a corner, head bowed and hands trembling.

"What's up, Bob?" I asked, leaning where the light of our eyes could mingle.

"We were best mates, padre. Lived in the same street, went to the same school, joined the same mob, and came over with the BEF."

A molten tear dripped down his nose and I mentally took my sandals off, aware I was on holy ground.

"When it went sour, we headed towards Dunkirk."

I touched his shoulder lightly.

"The bloody world exploded as a shell knocked us flat. Scrambling up, I heard this pathetic whimpering and looked to see where it was coming from…" His eyes screwed up in the agony of ancient memories, "Donovan's wounds were terrible, red and open."

The singing was rattling glasses. From the corner of my eye, I noticed that some of the lads were realising that Bob was laying ghosts. Tommy gave me a "do your stuff, padre" nod, before turning to divert attention away from our hallowed place in the crowded room.

"Donovan was so badly wounded they couldn't get morphine into him. This M.O. [medical officer] took me by the shoulders."

"Son, I'll not hide it from you: he's in agony. His mother and Lord aside, you know him better than anyone. Can you think of anything to ease his passing?"

A round of applause erupted. A moment's silence, then the singing started again. The Ukrainians were winning–but our lot didn't know. They were having such a good time that neither party cared.

"I got as close as I dared", Bob continued, "His flesh was so raw I couldn't touch him. Before I knew it, my lips started singing a song we'd known. Others followed until his breathing fell silent and I knew he'd gone. Can you imagine singing a friend to death?"

We didn't get to Manchester Hill next day. No one minded when I took padre's privilege and diverted to Dunkirk. Bob and I stood by Donovan's grave while a true and good friend said his fond farewell to a boyhood pal.

Bob lightened on the ferry and headed for the bar for quality time with his mates before the White Cliffs of Dover came into view.

The last time I saw him, Bob, who looked youthful in a new bomber jacket, he had a woman on his arm.

"Hi, padre!" he greeted cheerfully. "Will you marry us?"

It's astonishing what we can pick up once we have laid old burdens down. Perhaps the road back to lost youth really can be located in the magic of soul lifting, memory stirring music.

2009 Poppy Appeal

We think of history as in the past, but personal, family, national and global history is being made every day. As president of Belle Vue Royal British Legion (RBL), I attended Belle Vue Barracks as the guest of Joe and Carol Larrigan, two of the vertebrae in our branch backbone, for the award ceremony for cadets who'd helped the 2009 Poppy Appeal.

Having just posted a letter to Lord Lieutenant Warren J. Smith Esq. JP in relation to a bash at the end of The Mall later in the year, it was good to see him arrive in person to make the presentations. The mess hall bulged with members of the chain gang, including Manchester Lord Mayor Alison Frith, various military and civilian dignitaries and a VIP lineup of Army, Air and Sea Cadets.

Following an Act of Remembrance, RBL County Manager, Martin Watkins gave a statistical take on the historic development of this ceremony: The first competition in 1996 saw Greater Manchester raise £8,600 towards the national poppy appeal. The 2009 total was thirteen times that amount. Interestingly, the total in 2006 had been six and a half times that collected in 1996, while 2009's total was twice that and 36% up on 2008.

Taking the period of remembrance as fourteen days, every minute of that period, between them, our cadets had collected the equivalent of the hourly national minimum wage. In keeping with recent years, Greater Manchester had collected the highest amount nationally: £112,505.54. Greater Manchester assistant Chief Constable, ex-Naval officer, Terry Sweeney, spoke of his pride in our young people; while the Lord Lieutenant who–like his predecessor, John Timms, also present,–clearly leads by example.

Armistice Day at Heroes Wood: The Kennedy family, co-founders, with the author, of Gorton Pagan Moot.

Warren spoke of collecting with cadets and being saddened to note members of his own generation lowering their heads and hurrying by.

He had, however, been heartened at the enthusiasm of students and other young people who approached to buy poppies.

Next, starting with the senior service and moving through Army to Air Cadet Squadrons, presentations were made to the top three units in each of the services, with additional awards to the most improved units (well done Belle Vue!!!) and top individual collectors.

Appreciation was expressed for Kingston Interiors efforts in raising contributions for the Poppy Appeal within the Muslim community.

Finally, a personal thank you from me to a certain woman whose late partner had been special forces–you know who you are–for the bottle of whiskey you kindly brought to my home earlier in the evening. Walking into the barracks with a bottle of alcohol bulging from my pocket may have reinforced some people's stereotype of the clergy, but I assure you it was placed into the capable hands of Cadet Officer Bashir–who can be trusted to share it. Can't she? She can, can't she?

Taffy and Wilf

Gail Spelman's invitation to attend an unveiling ceremony at Philips Park on Sunday 24th July led my eyes towards the SAS beret in my office display cabinet.

Taffy was in his eighties when his picture was shown to police officers with the warning, "If this gentleman is being attacked, do not intervene without his invitation."

This followed an incident in which officers, having spotted a frail old gentleman about to be beaten up by three muggers, hurried across the road to his assistance. By the time they'd got over, the muggers were sprawled at Taffy's feet. The officer who tapped him on the shoulder to ask if he was ok was sharply elbowed unconscious for his concern.

A Barnardo's Boy, Taffy transferred from the Welsh Borderers to the SAS during the Second World War, teaching himself magic in lulls between actions.

Wilf was a Manchester Regiment old boy whose duties as a post-war SAS 'pilgrim' included walking Burma's railway lines alone with a spade to bury the dead and guarding Spandau Prison's lone Nazi occupant, Rudolph Hess. Wilf wouldn't call in the middle of the night to ask me to meet him without reason.

The headlights flashed twice, signalling me to park up behind Philips Park Cemetery, where Wilf and fellow King's-men were waiting.

"What's up?"

"We were down the mess this afternoon and someone told Taffy vandals had desecrated war graves here and the VC [Victoria Cross] plaques could be nicked. He said he'd come tonight and shoot the buggers. He won't if he sees his padre."

We scrambled over the wall and made our way through the cemetery until we heard voices. As we moved out of the shadows near the chapel, Taffy was chatting to a group of lads like old mates.

"Bugger me, what you lot doing here?" We were too late. He'd shot every one of them–with his camera.

"Just explaining to the boys here that these graves represent lads like themselves who did amazing things for the freedom they enjoy. They've promised not to mess with this place again, whether or not I use the photographs I've taken of them tonight. What say we take them on a battlefield pilgrimage so they get the bigger picture?"

A few days later, I arranged for Wilf, myself and some of the lads to meet here again–in daylight with members of the city council. We suggested that the VC plaques be taken down and stored until they could be returned at safer times. All these years on, it's grand to be invited to see that done. Standing alongside local school children, relatives of Rorke's Drift defenders, fellow British Legionnaires, King's-Men and members of the Royal Welsh Regiment, to watch Lord Lieutenant Warren Smith unveil stones commemorating Private Jones VC, Private Stringer VC, Lodge and Lyons (Rorke's Drift), and Brown and Richardson (Charge of the Light Brigade), I'll think of warriors like Taffy, Wilf and others beloved who've gone to meet their kings.

Bring 'em Home

The saying: "who strikes first has already lost" suggests that any act of aggression is a form of self-harm. It came to mind when my son rang to say he'd met an old mate in town not long out of the army with nowhere to go.

"Leave it with me."

Remembering homeless men from the 1980s who hadn't slept in a bed since being demobbed at the end of the Second World War, until our Lifeshare teams went out to find and bring them back into society's hearth glow, I thought it wouldn't take long to sort a bivouac. But it had been a good few years and Manchester's landscape had changed dramatically. The direct access centre we'd campaigned for to replace old flea-ridden hostels had been demolished; another hostel had been instructed to close one floor with the loss of forty beds and not take anyone until its figures dropped below 80, which was weeks away.

Time after time I hit a wall. There's no priority for single men, even those who've risked their lives to protect their country or the civilians of a foreign land. Saying a prayer, I tried one last shot. I rang a place that had sheltered me in a Lancashire town when I'd been homeless years before. Bingo!

With a nose-bag Kate had made them, I set off to pick Steven and his pal up in Manchester. As we drove up the motorway, I put the radio on. As if on cue, Bruce Springsteen started to sing a song from his

Seeger Years album, *If you love this Land of the Free, bring 'em home.* My eyes filled with tears as the young man beside me started to sob uncontrollably.

Memories of Sally Adams, a member of the Federation of Allied Combatants, and her husband, Ben, came to my mind. Ben, you see, had become something of an icon of the British soldier. Ben Adams, after fibbing about his age, had joined up to help his dad during the First World War. He was fourteen. Ben went on to serve in the army through both world wars and more. After he left, Ben was either a Terrier or teaching band music to cadets. His must be the record–for one way or another Ben, who lived with his wife, Sally, in Gorton, was connected to the British Army for some eighty years.

British soldier, Ben Adams, with his father at start of the First World War.

Our 'darling girls and boys' don't have to serve that long to have put their lives in danger to hold the freedom the rest of us enjoy.

It struck me that night that our government is now sending our troops on several fronts, while at home they are devastating the very resources they will need to get back on their feet when they come home. How very dare they! In this ninetieth year since the forming of the Royal British Legion, it's about time we called to account those who, from their personal comfort zones, send our children into danger and then abandon them when they have done their duty. It really won't do anymore.

Antiques and Other Storytelling Methods

When BBC TV's *Antiques Roadshow* visited Manchester Town Hall, Elaine and I was pleased to meet with good neighbours and friends from across the city. Like us, most knew their prized possessions were of little monetary value, but were happy to gain fresh insights into family or community history.

My office is filled with antique and retro curios. When someone comes in need of a chat, I offer them a tray and suggest that while I make them a brew, they might like to explore and place five objects on the tray that draw their interest. This enables the conversation to open up when the time comes for them to tell their own story, for personal stories are often hard to access, let alone articulate. So, having taken along a few items gathered on battlefield pilgrimages as a veterans' padre over the years–a First World War artillery fuse; SS Pamir bosun's whistle; phials of sand collected from the Normandy beaches on the 60th anniversary of D-Day and a porcelain poppy porcine–I was delighted to be invited to take part in an *Antiques Roadshow*/Royal British Legion special on military history, at the National Memorial Arboretum later in the year.

As featured on my radio show on 6th April, in its 90th Anniversary year, the RBL is gathering stories from ex-military folk; resistance fighters and refugees relating to conflicts from the Second World War to the present.

Other stories that are important include tales of the lives of ordinary men and women in industry, leisure, sport and the arts. For years I've held that some of the best stories of ordinary people who achieve or experience extraordinary things remain untold.

Having been privileged to learn many wonderful real-life tales over the years, it's been my pleasure to share some of them through my *Looking Back* newspaper column and radio show.

One reason such stories remain hidden is that not being about the rich and famous they don't attract funding, so I write my column and present the radio show voluntarily in order to be able to tell the stories of real people, which are so important to posterity.

Just as the *Antiques Roadshow* affords valuable and often entertaining glimpses into bygone times, so do our public libraries, local history groups, community radio and local papers. All play a valuable part in keeping alive the stories of Manchester's families and neighbourhoods.

Columns like *Manchester Evening News' In-Touch* page have helped numerous people get back in contact with long-lost family members, ex-school pals, old comrades or colleagues from bygone workplaces. If you've never used such services, you may not fully appreciate how valuable they can be to those delving deeper into their own identity.

When times are hard and those in power are seeking to make spending cuts, ordinary people need to stand together to ensure that local resources are not taken away from our communities. One way of doing this is simply to make maximum use of them.

The Night That Santa Called

When, as a guest on her 2009 Christmas Eve show on BBC Radio Manchester, Becky Want, asked for my favourite Christmas memory. 'Snowy' immediately sprang to mind.

Like many of his generation who had put their lives on the line for freedom, Snowy had been promised a country fit for heroes at the end of the Second World War. In reality, his home and family ties had been destroyed during the Blitz. His job gone to someone else, Snowy followed a stream of old soldiers into the ranks of the homeless. By the time I met him in the mid-eighties, he'd been sleeping rough for over thirty-five years.

Always clean, he and other ex-service friends in the same boat used the drop-in-centres to maintain their appearance. Ironically this meant they were never believed when they presented for the 'No-Fixed-Abode' allowance, so they gave up trying. "We survived the battlefields of Europe", Snowy once told me, when asked if he wanted us to help him find a place to live, "We won't accept hand-outs in our own land."

One mid-December evening, I spotted Snowy while driving back from the university with the mini-bus we borrowed for the night-time soup runs. He was killing time before our visit to the 'half-door' skipper in an external lift shaft that he shared with two other old soldiers.

"Fancy a brew, Snowy?" I asked. "Hop in."

Climbing on board thinking we were off to a café, Snowy was somewhat surprised when we stopped outside a house.

"I can't go in there", he complained, "what would the owner say?"

"He says you are most welcome, Snowy. This is my house."

Snowy didn't get his nickname for nothing. His hair was thick and white. Being winter he'd grown a bushy beard to keep his face warm. When our small children saw him sitting in an armchair by the fire with a cup of tea and a mince pie, they were in no doubt who this visitor was. They played happily at his feet and climbed into his lap. For years after they would talk about the day Santa came to see them personally.

Snowy came back to town with us when Elaine and I took the children for a drive through Manchester's Christmas Lights; each giving him a huge hug as he climbed out. As we waved goodbye, I shouted that I'd see him later. By the time we met during soup run that evening, Snowy had been thinking.

"Dave", he said, "I rather think it's time I settled down again."

The last time I saw Snowy, he was coming home from the pub just down his street. We met at his front door. "By heck, lad" he murmured, "I'm right glad you persuaded me to get a house."

"I'm right glad you decided the time had come", I told him. I'm also glad that my children saw you for the hero you truly are, so good night, Santa", I joked as we gave each other a huge hug.

The War and Peace Paradox

Among accounts of monkish military antics comes a tale of a fighting friar who, while the provisioner for an Anglo-Saxon people's militia, found himself aboard a small sailing vessel pursued by two warships.

Ordering a tack into the wind, he instructed a group of sailors to bear sacks of lime to the tops of the rigging and, after covering their faces, to release them as the enemy ships homed in, thus blinding their pursuers and enabling his ship to make its escape.

Besides deepening prayer and meditation in the world, Buddhist, Christian and other religious orders have left a legacy of martial arts and ale. Paradoxically, men and women of faith, promoters of peace, are often found among the finest conflict resolution strategists and bravest warriors.

Jesus, often called 'Prince of Peace', possessed remarkable strategic timing. References in scripture depict him as fully aware that one day he'd be called to lay down his life. Luke 4, 28-30 gives an example of his ninja-like ability to move unharmed through a crowd bent on destroying him, thus evading death until a moment he would chose to complete his ministry.

Belle Vue Barracks, in Gorton, once housed an SAS Territorial Army unit.

When 'Phantom Major' David Stirling founded the Special Air Service, alongside the Israeli Army Group (IAG) to help bring the Second World War to a conclusion and reduce the endless slaughter, the bible to hand was the King James. One SAS blazer badge bears the legend: "Matthew 22, 9". The verse reads: "Go ye therefore into the highways, and as many as ye shall find, bid to the marriage", a reference to that feast in heaven that marks the end of conflict and the seal of peace.

Consisting of Jewish combatants who had a vested interest in ending the war to save their people, the IAG risked torture and death on capture. Nevertheless, they and the SAS, along with Muslim allies, went out into the highways where, instead of targeting German soldiers' lives, they destroyed fuel and ammo dumps that were keeping the Nazi war machine mighty.

Their valour helped bring the North Africa campaign to a conclusion, releasing energy for D-Day and the liberation of Europe.

Stirling, a Christian, showed how a small number of cooperating, risk-taking peace seekers willing to lay down their lives for the peace of the world, could do more to defeat an army than whole battalions. A favourite regimental hymn associated with John Bunyan led to SAS soldiers being called 'Pilgrims'. Like Jesus' strong man guarding his home, they were not formed to wage war for war's sake, but to protect. While some spurn the infantry hymn, *O Valiant Heart*, many–including some whose chosen way was violence–enjoy their hold on life because others who do not at all like war have learned its ways and, being gentle as doves, are as cunning as foxes.

PART 6

OTHER STORIES OF WOUNDED HEALERS

Agatha Christmas

When *Hercule Poirot's Christmas* cropped up on the reading list for our Sunday book club, snow-dusted memories were stirred of a Christmas some three or four decades previously, when the spirit of *Poirot's* creator, Agatha Christie, played a part in solving a Christmas mystery.

Before I begin, let me tell you about Oggy, whose spirit is part of this telling too. When we met many years ago, he had only recently recovered from a horrific incident when his motorcycle was hit by a car speeding across a junction whose driver was certainly not following the think bike mantra.

Oggy's left arm was in a permanent metal frame, his legs spindly due to atrophy accrued during months on life support, and his face was locked in a mischievous grin. Oggy had been something of a lad before his accident, from which he was not expected to recover. Following his remarkable comeback, even his sisters, who were to become like family to me too, were surprised at the change in his personality.

Oh, he was still mischievous–but there were other qualities at play and he was to spend the remainder of his life lifting up and empowering others.

My infant son had not long made a remarkable comeback too. Richard was one of twenty-five babies across Wales and North-West England who had been struck by a virus that left a toxin in their systems that was slowly closing life down. He was the only one to survive, albeit in a profoundly handicapped body. He had come back to us, though, with a cosmic sense of humour and though he couldn't speak, he was able to commune in ways at which even his doctors marvelled. It was as if he had been to the other side of the universe, across cusps of life and death, and was struck dumb by the awe of what he had experienced. As soon as I met Oggy, I knew he had that same gift and we became immediate friends.

"This is Steve", said project manager, Lorraine, as she introduced us.

Lorraine wanted me to know that the National Children's Home partnership with Piccadilly Radio, for which I had just volunteered, had other male counsellors, though the vast majority were women.

"Call me Oggy", Steve had said.

"Oggy will be your buddy as you develop your skills", Lorraine had stated. "Your mental health and homelessness background will give you some grounding, but we operate by Rogerian principles that involve deep listening skills, a totally putting aside of self and all our stereotypes and judgements to focus on the people who will call us in times of personal crisis."

Over the next few months, Oggy helped to develop in me an ability to switch all else off so that I could give full focus to people calling our service, skills that would come in useful as a negotiator working alongside armed forces and emergency services many years later. He was a mentor again when I and others set up the Lifeshare charity to take that non-judgmental, listening approach to homeless people and trafficked women and children on the streets of Manchester and Salford. He was there to spell me alternate years running Piccadilly Radio and then Granada TV's Christmas Toy and Tin Appeals; there leading the welfare rights and advocacy team when I was called on to manage a negotiating team on behalf of prisoners and their families during the Strangeways Prison riots.

It wasn't all counselling and response. We helped manage a heavy metal band, met socially and developed a wicked ability to bounce things off each other without verbal communication whenever it was 'game on' and we were winding someone up.

From the get-go, Oggy was with me even when we were not together, such as that Christmas when the call of which I write came in. It had been Oggy who had suggested, when Lifeshare was strong with premises and paid workers, that we who had volunteered from the start might now seek paid work in roles where our insights may prove useful.

He was right. What we had learned about trauma, sexual politics and disadvantage as we helped men demobbed at the end of the Second World War find homes and even start their own businesses after years of rough sleeping, or while empowering women with self-confidence and belief. These insights could be applied to reduce people in at-risk groups becoming homeless or being sexually exploited.

While Oggy specialised in Welfare Rights, others became probation, police or prison officers. Some of our women helped develop safe house networks for prostitutes and other trafficked people. We all stayed in touch, calling on one another's specialities–such as when my role as a war generation padre enabled us to access the skills of resistance fighters who had got Jewish children and British airmen to safety under the radar of the hostile Nazi regime, skills that helped us develop anti-trafficking strategies. You can imagine how useful that was during international sporting events when thousands of women and girls are trafficked by criminal gangs who know that many men away from home have more money than conscience.

I'd decided that as well as the armed forces community, the other high-risk group I wanted to get alongside were young people leaving the care of local authorities, who back then were often left to fend for themselves from the age of sixteen, often becoming prey to pimp, paedophile and pusher predators. They also faced a high risk of homelessness. Of course, we all got behind developing the 1989 Children Act to try and ensure local authorities acted more compassionately and responsibly, and in due course, I was one of the original social workers laying down leaving care services across local authorities.

That Christmas, when the call came in, I was simply doing a shift in a residential setting for young people preparing for independence. The caller knew the number from his own years in the care of that local authority and he just wanted to say goodbye to the world and thought whoever was on duty at the last place he had felt safe was as good a person as anyone to receive his goodbye message.

Realising I had a person intent on suicide who was planning to hang himself from a tree in a place where he had spent some of his childhood years, all the skills that Oggy had helped develop in me came into play. This is not the place to outline the various ways we worked towards a solution. Let's just say finding our common ground was an important part of how things unfolded.

Having established that this was the worse Christmas my caller had ever experienced following the unravelling of personal relationships topped by aching loneliness, I explored what experiences he was comparing it with, encouraging him to talk about happier Christmas memories.

What did he enjoy when life was good? Did he like movies or play sports? Did he enjoy a good read, and if so, what? That's when we discovered our shared enjoyment of Agatha Christie novels.

"Did you know *Miss Marple* was probably named for Marple Village?" He did not.

"Did you know Agatha Christie spent childhood Christmases at Abney Hall, now managed by the local authority you work for?" I did not.

He got quite animated telling me how special that place was. In the end, it was not a vast leap of empathy to surmise that this was the location his footsteps would take him once our conversation ended. Was this where he had previously secreted the ladder and rope, he had mentioned with which he intended to create his exit strategy?

Quickly scrawling a note for a colleague to use another line to contact emergency services, I kept my caller talking, seeking his views on Agatha Christie stories and asking whether he'd ever read Edgar Allan Poe's detective stories, begun in Poe's efforts to solve a real crime, which went on to set the standard for a now-established genre. Slowly, I was beginning to develop a rapport. He was interested to learn that Poe had particularly influenced Arthur Conan Doyle, creator of *Sherlock Holmes*. This proved a useful talking point, for another building in my employer's network was on Baker Street. This resulted in his desire to talk further. Some years later while working out of Baker Street, I'd put Room 221B on my office door and had my mail addressed to Room 221B Baker Street, much to the amusement of some colleagues and the annoyance of others who hadn't thought of it first.

At last, my caller had said all he wanted to say. Knowing we could not be absolutely certain my hunch was right, I thanked him for a most stimulating conversation, adding: "I wish you'd change your mind. It would be good to get a chance to meet and talk further."

"It's been good to chat", he'd replied. "But what must be must be."

As the phone went dead, I wondered if between myself, my colleague and the first responders we'd done enough. As I picked up the mug of tea my colleague had made, my hands were trembling.

"You did the best you could", she said. "We just have to wait and see…" The ringing of the phone cut her short.

"We're with him", said a local police officer who sometimes called in for a brew. "Think we were just in time. Leave him to us now. We'll ensure he gets the help he needs."

When the director of social services asked if I could do an extra shift in the early New Year, it seemed odd that the request was not coming through my line manager. Nevertheless, I agreed to do the shift. I'd been on duty a couple of hours, when my colleague responded to the doorbell and moments later was admitting the police officer who was wont to pop in for brews.

"How do, buggerlugs!" I greeted.

In response to the question that hung between us, he pushed the door fully open to reveal a man standing nervously behind him.

"You two need to renew your conversation", the policeman said as he followed my colleague into the kitchen. No need for me to ask–no need for him to say. We looked at each other before meeting mid-hallway in a tearful hug.

So glad he made it through that night. So proud that he went on to become one of the wounded healers who are still out there helping others through the dark terrain of mental ill-health, loneliness and isolation. He seemed a far more contented and wiser man than he had been when he'd made that Christmas phone call.

The last time I saw him he was working out of a project that was helping people appeal cruel Department for Work and Pensions 'austerity' decisions that had driven them to the brink of suicide. His ability to keep them buoyant, hopeful, determined and–alive!–was well established.

It seemed to me a little bit of cosmic serendipity that not long before my good friend Oggy had died–I did his funeral a couple of years ago in a cemetery not far from Abney Hall, where Agatha Christie had spent so many childhood Christmases–the young man who had called that night was active in a project that Oggy had helped to establish as part of his legacy in the world.

Paying the Ferryman

Lent is a time for followers of the Way of the Cross to examine anew all personal assumptions, fears, prejudices; all aspects of our ego. It is, in a way, and approached with sincerity, a wilderness time when, following the example of the one who goes ahead of us, we delve deep into our own psyche to remember who we are, so that we may better be ourselves, become a better version of ourselves as we move through the cycle of the seasons.

In this process, we struggle with our perceptions of what it might be to be powerful, wealthy or famous. We must do this anew as we make our pilgrimage afresh through every year, looking towards the sorrowful journey through the passion to the great feast that we celebrate with Pagans and others as Easter.

Each year is a pilgrimage. Each faith has its own approaches, frameworks and understandings. For Christians, Lent is akin to Ramadan, or perhaps Haj for our Muslim cousins.

So, some personal things I have been touched by during Lent 2023:

- Taking inanimate things for granted. Having been without a car for a few days and likely to be without one for a few days more as it undergoes major surgery, I've come to appreciate what a helpful companion it actually is.
- A renewed and deepened appreciation for bus and taxi drivers who have been there to help me plan my journeys around Lancashire, Cheshire and Yorkshire in order to fulfil commitments to celebrate rites of passage for other people's joyful and sorrowful moments along their own life's journey.
- The kindness of those I support in supporting me back, like the Cheshire Regiment lad who drove me home this evening after I'd caught two busses to reach his home to help plan a funeral.
- A reminder that we are exactly where we are meant to be, with or without the resources we would hope to ideally have in a given situation.

Just as Elaine and I were finishing our evening meal, which we had begun on time thanks to that Cheshire lad, one of those calls to be on the holy ground of a soul's crossing life's threshold.

"My grandad is dying…"

"Tell him to hang on, I'm on foot."

Snatching up a bible, a bottle of holy water, a crucifix and a stole. I get a cab to the nursing home. I don't look like a priest without my dog collar, wearing a fisherman's woolly jumper against the cold, but my community know me and the nursing staff hurry me through.

The granddaughter is waiting at the top of the corridor. She guides me to the room where other family members cluster around the bed. I place my hat on a young man's head, put the stole over my shoulder and crouch to take the wrinkled, blood-blistered hand and begin the three-way conversation, laced with familiar words, to reach this loved, lived man while inviting the divine presence to make itself tangible for all of us–but especially for him.

Only moments, so as not to encroach on the last opportunity of his loved ones to say farewell, then out into the night to walk home.

As I emerge from a side street onto Gorton Lane, the corporation yard (it will ever be that to me) looms into view, and I think of another soul, long associated with that place, who, not a million miles away, is waiting to pay the ferryman. I make a conscious note to have my own pennies ready. You never know when the river will need to be crossed.

It's a lonely place near the banks in the darkness, but just a few paces away, on either side of the river, there is welcome, light, love, peace and unfathomable joy.

Leaf and Lizzie

Lizzie Andrews was a feisty, rebellious young teenager who dyed her hair bright blue and told her mum she wanted a tattoo. Lizzie had become the mascot of big, burly bikers who only had to think of her to feel inspired. They adored her. But then, Lizzie was adorable.

There was, though, more to Lizzie than met the eye, for she was living with cystic fibrosis (CF). In fact, she was arguably dying of CF. The only thing that could tip the balance towards living with CF was a lung transplant, and Lizzie wanted this more than she wanted that tattoo.

My mate, Big Andy, told me about Lizzie and how she wanted to raise awareness about the CF community and encourage more people to become organ donors.

"Can you interview her on your Punk Monk show?" He asked.

When I spoke with Lizzie and her mum Rachel on the phone, the pair were really looking forward to doing the show. Having fallen in love with Lizzie's incredible enthusiasm and energy, I was really looking forward to meeting her.

Unlike most parents, but sadly like virtually all parents who had a child with CF, Rachel had worked with the medical support network to help her child plan her own funeral. Few parents imagine having to do that. The fact was, though, without a transplant, children with CF rarely make it to adulthood. We were optimistic. Lizzie and Rachel; set a date and I was hoping to support this astonishingly brave child in her efforts to support other children with CF.

Big Andy and I met through Andrew Roughly, anchor for Roughley's Bike Show which, as well as putting an amazing annual bike show in Stockport with stalls, children's rides and bands on its truck stage, also organises annual Egg Runs at Easter and Toy Runs at Christmas to bring cheer to children spending the holiday in Francis House and Together Trust Hospices. Hundreds of bikers, trikers and scooter riders take part in these events, many dressed as easter chicks, bunnies, Santa, elves or fairies to make the children smile. It is such a joy to witness the excitement of the children when they hear the bikes arriving and to watch the bikers like big kids themselves asking the kids if they can take a look at their mobility scooters or wheelchairs in exchange for a sit on a Harley or a Royal Enfield. I've been going on the egg and toy runs and attending the bike show for years. They are the highlights of my year.

Bikers who take part have big hearts. But big hearts can lead to big tears. A number of times I've stood near a biker on their second run asking where the kids are that they met on their first run, and listened as silence descended to give them time to work it. Then they'd turn and find a quiet corner where, shoulders heaving, the tears would flow as they realised exactly what hospices are about. But when Big Andy phoned to say Lizzie wouldn't be doing the show and mum wondered whether I'd help celebrate her life at her funeral, we both went into meltdown.

When the day came to do Lizzie's funeral, the streets were lined with children and teachers from her school, friends and neighbours and a cavalcade of bikers escorted the cortege. Like many others, I had dyed my hair and beard blue in honour of this amazing child.

'Leaf' was in the very same circumstances as Lizzie. Indeed, the two girls were friends. Unlike Lizzie, Leaf was matched with a donor. She and her mum, Drou, came on my show later in the year to help take Lizzie's intentions forward and in due time we saw a change in the law that meant people had to opt out of being donors rather than sign up to be donors to increase the chances of life carrying forward. Along the way, in Lizzie's memory, hundreds signed up to become organ donors.

GAP

Listeners rang in to say how moving they had found it to hear Leaf describe how she saw her donor as her angel, and the lungs she had donated as her angel wings.

It is very difficult for a child with CF to breathe. "Breathe Easy!" has become a phrase in the CF community of sufferers, their families and medical professionals for wishing someone well. The thing is, when Leaf could finally breathe easy, she realised something she had previously had no way of knowing: she could sing. Her voice is as beautiful as her soul is gorgeous, and she has become a gifted performer, writing songs that many–from ex-PM, Tony Blair, to *Doctor Who* star, David Tennant; guitar maestro and British music ambassador, Aziz Ibrahim, to audiences up and down the land, have been deeply moved by. Then, just meeting Leaf herself can be a very moving and humbling experience.

Author (right) chilling with Dave Chi during Aziz Ibrahim's Roadhouse farewell gig.

While I love and respect every member of the CF community, who remind me of our own nine years with our amazing son whom we knew was unlikely to make adulthood for other health reasons, I have a special place in my heart for Lizzie and Leaf, ambassadors both for a community that is one of the bravest, wisest, kindest networks of people it has been my privilege to know. Namaste, brave souls all.

The Anglesey Angel

In the 1980s, Lifeshare was training some 200 volunteers each year, about a quarter of them students from Manchester University. Between them, our outreach workers had a vast range of skills. A Chinese student who had been inspired by his lifelong connection with martial arts to study physics. As well as helping on the soup runs and outreach teams, he would gather volunteers and homeless people together in spaces like Piccadilly Gardens and Crowcroft Park to lead health-enhancing Tai Chi sessions in the early dawn. Others used their skills and experience to help homeless people reconnect with their own half-forgotten skills or teach them new ones as they supported them in developing their own businesses. By the early 1990s, there were at least three popular restaurants that had started when volunteers and homeless people used the Lifeshare kitchen to make sandwiches, which were sold from mobile displays carried on straps like a cinema usherettes' tray in office blocks, back street garages and other places where workers needed to source breakfast or lunch. Such simple approaches gave people the skills and confidence to take up training in health and hygiene; catering and business skills. Our approach was a far cry from the one size fits all street magazine that later became so popular.

Simply having the eyes of so many people with empathy out on the streets was making changes in awareness that were increasing understanding and leading to changes in public attitude. Sometimes, this was accomplished due to the personal risks that not only our volunteers, but others supporting our efforts were willing to take.

We would spend hours each day in Piccadilly bus station bathing the feet of homeless people, whose toenails had grown under their feet to form a hard hoof that was excruciatingly painful to walk on. Once the feet had been softened by regular bathing, using salt washes and cider vinegar, we were, at last, able to trim the toenails and remove the hoof, improvising for dressings with thick, soft socks that, changed every day, helped feet to heal. Present-day readers must understand that back then, so strong was the denial from both central and local government that our cities and even towns hid large populations of rough sleepers; so ingrained were the prejudices against them, that it was close to impossible to register people with a GP, dentist or optician, let alone a chiropodist. Through Lifeshare at Christmas, we learned to tap into the seasonal tsunami of goodwill to get entertainers, hairdressers, doctors, nurses and other skilled professionals to take part in our annual winter shelter initiative that helped feed the homeless, while offering them a range of health, well-being and other opportunities to break cycles that disempowered them. As the medical community realised the extent of the problem, they responded lovingly and projects like Manchester Action of Street Health (MASH) became an ally alongside our own outreach approaches.

Another major breakthrough came when Carol spotted two eleven-year-old girls at a bus stop one night.

"David, they've been there a while and every bus that stops there has come and gone", she told me. "They're not properly dressed for this weather. I think they are runaways."

Then, as now, young people run away from home or care for a variety of reasons.

As Carol and I walked back towards them, they were talking to a middle-aged man with a guitar case. He was telling them how they could sneak in through the back and spend the night in the warmth of his hotel room.

"Hiya, girls!" Carol said in her gravelly, motherly voice. "You okay?"

"They're fine", the man said. "I'll sort them out."

"Girls", I said, ignoring him. "Whatever your issues are, we can help you get somewhere safe to stay tonight. I'm sure you'll realise the irony of me telling you that accepting help from strangers is a huge risk. This man is a stranger, but we are strangers too. Which of us you decide to trust is up to you..."

"Oh, I'm sorry, I've got to go", said guitar man, and he rushed off under Carol's knowing gaze. For every volunteer we could field, there was a pimp, a paedophile and a pusher trying to reach the same disaffected kids.

The girls confided that they were friends who had run away to Manchester because there were unresolved issues back home that they felt their respective parents were unwilling to address. While Carol and the women on that night's team gave them a hot meal in the back of the mini-bus, I nipped to a phone box to make a call. Irene worked for National Children's Home (NCH). In my role with Careline, we'd been talking recently about the plight of young runaways.

We were concerned that in those days, nobody seemed to ask what they were running from and police usually told them not to be so naughty and took them right back to where they'd run from.

"Look, what I'm going to ask you is risky. It could even cost you your job, but I know and trust you and you live in an all-female household…"

When I told her about the girls and my promise to find them somewhere safe for tonight, Irene realised that between us we were taking society across a threshold.

"I'll make up their beds", she said.

After calling the police to tell them that the girls were safe should anyone report them missing and that we had agreed to meet them the next day and negotiate a return home, I dropped them off at Irene's and, after dropping the volunteers off, drive home.

As I parked outside the house, there was a police car parked there waiting. I walked across and asked its two occupants if they wanted an early morning brew. As we sat with our hot mugs, the senior officer, a sergeant, stated his position: "After you rang us, we contacted the parents. They insist that their daughters are taken home tonight, so unless you tell us where they are, I'm afraid we will have to arrest you."

"They didn't report them missing until the police got in touch, then insisted they go home tonight?" I reflected back. "Sergeant, these girls told us they have run away previously. Did anyone report them missing on those occasions?"

My backup came from an unexpected source.

"He's right, Sarge", the young constable stated. "Remember that course you sent me on? We were told that for every child who is reported to have run away, there are two whom nobody bothers reporting."

"If we break our promise and they are returned home without anybody listening to what they have to say, next time they run away they won't trust people like us", I pleaded. "You know the circumstances in which we met them. What might guitar man be up to now had they gone with him?"

The sergeant looked at me for a long moment.

"Let me make a call", he said at last.

After speaking with that night's shift inspector, he turned back to me.

"Okay. You need some sleep and I guess they do too", he said. "Here's the number of the inspector who'll be on duty in the morning.

When I'm next on shift, I'm expecting to hear that you rang him and that these girls will have been spoken to by social services before a decision is made as to when and whether they are returned home."

The next day, I rang Irene. The girls had slept well and were ready to talk about their issues. I spoke with them long enough to gain their consent to let the police know where they were and wished them well.

Within days, Irene and I had called a meeting to discuss the issue of young runaways. As well as her own NCH organisation, we had invited Greater Manchester Police, the Association of Greater Manchester Authorities (AGMA), social services and the Children's Society. After outlining the issues, we suggested that approaches to runaway children needed to shift to empower children to speak up about what was going on for them rather than be treated as naughty and simply sent back. Remembering myself in a juvenile court on my way into the care system unable to express to adults who were sure they knew what was troubling me facts that may have helped them understand the impact of predatory adults like Brady and maybe even catch them before they were enabled to impact other lives, I laid out proposals for a listening, non-judgemental approach akin to the Rogerian model that was the basis of Careline and Lifeshare's way of working.

When we spoke about the need for children to feel confident talking about any brutality or bullying they may have experienced, or issues around sex and sexuality, a guy from the Children's Society made some very homophobic comments. As we'd been doing research into historic abuse within organised religion, Irene and I, along with most others around that table, realised that the Children's Society were perhaps unsuitable for this partnership due to their association with the Church of England. However, one of his female colleagues spoke out, pointing out that this problem was compounded by adult assumptions as to what was best and that maybe a time had come to listen to the children. She added a coded "and forbid them not" that caused her male colleague to hang his head in shame.

In the end, a pot of money was agreed and the Children's Society took the lead role as we established what came to be known as 'Safe in the City'.

People were still working on the Children Act, but the underpinning principle, "child's needs paramount", was at play. From then on, in Manchester at least, young runaways would be provided with safe havens where they would receive support to explore and address their issues with support from police and social services. As we anticipated, this reduced the risk of children themselves being criminalised, while enhancing opportunities to bring to book those who, often from positions of power and influence, were abusing their adult authority.

Some time had passed. Elaine and I had taken our children on holiday to Anglesey. We were on a bus heading for Llangefni to shop on the markets there. Behind us, we were vaguely aware of two young women in conversation. One seemed to be trying to support her friend in relation to an issue that was troubling her.

As we got up to go downstairs, I was cradling our handicapped son, Richard, while Elaine helped his sister and brothers negotiate the stairs.

"That's him!" a voice said behind me. "Maybe he'll know what to do."

Busy with Richard, I hadn't realised the remark was about me until we got off the bus and were getting the children organised and ready to go shopping.

"Hello", said a hesitant voice. "I looked up to see the young women, from the bus, gazing at me. "Do you remember me?"

"Oh, my goodness!" I responded. "Of course. How are you?" It was one of the two girls that Carol had spotted at a bus stop long ago.

"Well, thanks to you and your friends", I'm alright now. "The police took us home the next day, but they also arranged support. My friend is okay too."

"This is my wife, Elaine, and these are our children."

"This is another friend", she introduced her fellow bus traveller. I was deeply impressed when she had the maturity to ask her friend: "Is it okay if we tell him?"

Elaine took the children into the market so I could spend a few moments with the girls. The one I'd first met at a Piccadilly bus stop was a little older and wiser, as well as somewhat more confident in her own power now. Her friend had a problem, and she had been trying to persuade her not to do what she had done in a similar situation. I knew Manchester's networks like the back of my hand, but had little knowledge of support networks on Anglesey, but knew enough to know the local library could set them on the trail towards insightful projects on the island. They took my number with a promise to let me know how things worked out, though when I rejoined Elaine, I already knew, as subsequently proved the case, that yet another troubled lass had been diverted from potential disaster by having a friend who was herself, now, a wounded healer.

As for Carol, who set in motion events that changed the way young runaways are seen, she has remained a dear friend all these years on and I've come to know and respect her wonderful family.

Carol's husband, Wilf, decorated the premises when Lifeshare was, at last, able to move its kitchen and offices out of our family home into a newly renovated mill at 23 New Mount Street, near the Old Ragged School in Angel Meadow, which we shared with band, James, Mike Shaft's Sunset Radio, Body Positive and a fleet of projects and enterprises serving Manchester through art, music, self-help and more on the cusp of the 1980s and 90s.

Having done the groundwork to see the charity established, when we began to peel off to find paid work with vulnerable groups Carol, like me, went to work in children's homes, though she was in the private sector. Carol, Wilf and their sons took an interest in my role as a veterans' chaplain and we remained the sort of friends who may not see each other for ages, but could pick up where we had left off instantly when opportunities to meet arose.

When Wilf died, the family asked me to celebrate his life. A few years later, after my role as community coordinator restoring Gorton Monastery, I would marry one of Carol and Wilf's sons to his wonderful wife there. We're both long in the tooth now, but from time to time, I'll call round to annoy Carol and we'll chew the cud about the things we were up against to try and get society to better protect its children and look after its homeless people. Like all who spend their life's energies trying to fine-tune a society that is riddled with mistakes and assumptions, we often ask whether we did enough. Thing is, I can honestly say that Carol did all she could, while she can say the same about me, but it seems in the nature of a wounded healer never to be quite sure that they hadn't missed something really important.

PART 7

COMMENTS FROM OTHER WOUNDED HEALERS

Lisa Wild (*Lisbeth*)

Taken from my family as a child and labelled a difficult kid, I was locked away from society in a unit that became my home and school. The man who ran the place was seen as an expert on managing difficult children. Entrusted to look after me, under the noses of social service and education professionals, he instead abused me and controlled my silence using bribes and violence. It seemed as if this was normal life for a kid like me, and I felt powerless and unworthy of anything but his dreadful attention.

Then along came someone who believed in me and spoke up for me. At first bewildered, in time I felt worthy enough to expose my abusers pack of lies. My sense of unworthiness was replaced with self-confidence and I grew strong enough to take on the system that had abandoned me into the misery of an abuser's power. Raising my voice against the cruelty that had ignored my plight and that of other vulnerable children, my words became a powerful truth that cut through the clever arguments of a self-serving system like a hot knife through butter, revealing its arrogance, indifference and the deceit and conceit of its claimed expertise. Where once had been a frightened, compliant child, stood a warrior who could take on the monsters who were controlling other children like me.

Now, knowing I could achieve my own goals and succeed against whatever others stacked against me, I chose to harness the weapons of my hard gained knowledge and wisdom to stand as the fighter my own inner child had needed – **Lisa Wild (*Lisbeth*)**

Tom Rattigan

Anecdotes galore, with the reader wanting more! The author gives us another fascinating insight into his memorable life, whilst stirring up memories of Manchester. Poet, singer-songwriter, psychologist, author; ape keeper, ordained priest, speaker, radio-host and Punk Monk–to name just a few of his attributes! Behind each one is the same person, devoted to his calling and in my view, one of the kindest and gentlest of souls you'd care to meet.

I recall one of my first conversations with David, when he'd begged the question, "Is your father, one James [Jim] Rattigan?" to which I'd confirmed, "Indeed he is."

"One day, having looked after your dying father and coming to bury him, I knew I'd meet his son and be proud to do so."

"Was he dead at the time?" I'd cursedly asked.

"I believe so", was David's nonchalant reply!

There was no question from him, as to why I'd said such cruel sounding thing, and I knew at that precise moment that this was someone I could get on well with. Admittedly, I wasn't too sure what came with the 'Punk Monk' tag! I'd met quite a few punks in my own youth, my younger brother fronting the punk band 'State Victims'.

Punk Monk at Roughley's Bikeshow, featured on Stomping Ground's *Soldier* album

I'd assumed at the time Punk Monk was part of a rebellious era where anarchy, anti-authority, no dress sense, and showing one's admiration for a punk band by spitting at them, was the status-quo!

In David's case, accepting the honorarium 'Punk Monk' from Manchester musicians was an acknowledgement of years dealing with discontent, social decline and malaise caused by high inflation, unemployment, lack of care for the sick and the elderly, which the author passionately shows is still very much alive today.

Over time I got to know David and learned we had more than a sense of humour in common: we'd lived in and around Salford as kids during the early 60s; were published authors, poets and songwriters and, most telling, were both chosen by Ian Brady as potential victims. So, it wasn't surprising to me when we finally met in person for the first time on the set of the documentary, *Left for Dead,* that we both unquestionably accept that our own experiences pale significantly against the suffering of the bereaved families of the five known victims of the Moors Murderers.

When I greeted David in an embrace, I felt that same emotional guilt we were both destined to carry on our shoulders forever–**Tom Rattigan, author of *A slice of Jam and Bread***

ABOUT THE AUTHOR

Reverend David Gray is a Tau Interfaith Franciscan. He and his wife, Elaine, have several children and grandchildren and live in Sally-Manc land, as David likes to call the kissing cousin cities of Manchester and Salford, where he lives and works when not in his spiritual home of Alba, also known as Caledonia, the land to the north that Sassenachs call Scotland.

Spiritual servant leader of the Progressive Pagan-Christian Alliance, David was chaplain to First and Second World War veterans for many years, which led to his further training with One Spirit, the interfaith seminary that traces its roots back to the end of the Second World War, when priests, imams, rabbis and other spiritual and humanist leaders thought the world might benefit from a better understanding across the whole spectrum of human faith and cultural identity.

His other works include poetry and song lyrics for various bands and artists–he has appeared with several bands and is known as the Punk Monk on the Sally-Manc music scene.

David is also the author of *The Great Apes of Belle Vue*, which outlines his experience of communication with great apes and is available online and as hard copy in the shop at St. Francis Monastery in Gorton, which he helped to restore after years of dereliction.

As David Seagray, he has also written a grimoire novel for young adults: *All Hallowed*, which relates the adventures of *Pen*, a young witch, who, with her familiar *Moke*, helps unite the creatures, the living and the dead to fight corporate greed and global warming.

Further books in the *Pen and Moke* series are underway.

A member of Mensa, David's stepping stones to his present roles in life include training as a mental health and social work professional, founding the Lifeshare charity that works on the Sally-Manc margins, being a member of the magic circle, martial arts, a stand-up comedian, years as a radio presenter and as an inspirational speaker. He headed a negotiating team on behalf of prisoners' families during the 1990 Strangeways prison riots.

Printed in Great Britain
by Amazon